Mindfulness A to Z

D1468782

MINDFULNESS

108 INSIGHTS FOR AWAKENING NOW

Arnie Kozak, PhD

Wisdom

Wisdom Publications
199 Elm Street
Somerville, MA 02144 USA
wisdompubs.org

Library of Congress Cataloging-in-Publication Data
Kozak, Arnold, author.
  Mindfulness A to Z : 108 insights for awakening now / Arnie Kozak, Ph.D.
    pages cm
  ISBN 978-1-61429-057-5 (alk. paper) — ISBN 1-61429-057-1 (pbk. : alk. paper) —
ISBN 978-1-61429-069-8 (eBook)
  1. Meditation—Buddhism. I. Title.
  BQ5612.K68 2015
  294.3'4—dc23

                                   2015006366

ISBN 978-1-61429-057-5   ebook ISBN 978-1-61429-069-8

19 18 17 16 15
5   4   3   2   1

Cover design by Phil Pascuzzo. Interior design by Gopa&Ted2, Inc. Set in Fairfield LT
Std 45 Light 10.6/15.

"Present Tense" written by Eddie Vedder and Mike McCready, © 1996 Innocent
Bystander and Jumpin' Cat Music. Used by Permission. All rights reserved.
"The Jeweler" is from the Penguin publication *I Heard God Laughing, Renderings of
Hafiz,* © 1996 and 2006 Daniel Ladinsky and used with his permission

Wisdom Publications' books are printed on acid-free paper and meet
the guidelines for permanence and durability of the Production Guidelines
for Book Longevity of the Council on Library Resources.

This book was produced with environmental mindfulness. We have elected
to print this title on 30% PCW recycled paper. As a result, we have saved the
following resources: 16 trees, 7 million BTUs of energy, 1,394 lbs. of greenhouse
gases, 7,560 gallons of water, and 506 lbs. of solid waste. For more information
please visit our website, wisdompubs.org. This paper is also FSC certified.

Printed in the United States of America.

Please visit fscus.org.

Table of Contents

Preface

Mindfulness is about paying attention to our life as it unfolds, moment-by-moment. "To be mindful" is to bring a particular kind of attention to our experience—one that is keen and focused on what is actually happening, as opposed to what we wish would happen. Mindfulness privileges perception over imagination. At its deepest levels, developing mindfulness helps us to clearly see that we construct much of our experience of the world and ourselves. And by construct I mean the quality of our minds determines the quality of our experiences. We are "put together" by our beliefs, stories, and attitudes. By practicing mindfulness we can learn to relate to the world, others, and ourselves in a more open and accepting way, without so many preconditions for happiness. A serious commitment to mindfulness, practiced over time, can help to move us toward a more awakened way of being-in-the-world.

Mindfulness has been the central theme of my adult life; I make maintaining a mindful demeanor a daily aspiration. Though many days I fall short of my goal, the wonderful thing about life is that it offers us another chance to be mindful in the very next moment. Even lapses in mindfulness provide useful opportunities to develop our skill! The cultivation of mindfulness in the service of awakening is a lifelong endeavor.

This book is a field manual for awakening mindfulness within yourself. It is composed of 108 brief chapters that contain seeds of practical wisdom that you can cultivate in your life. The bits of wisdom collected in these pages are drawn from my decades of practicing mindfulness and are informed by my experience teaching mindfulness to clinical patients, members of the community, fellow health care practitioners, university students, and Buddhist seekers. Many of the entries contain personal stories; some of the entries are based on metaphors, a common literary form that the Buddha used in his teaching, and one that I explored more deeply in my book *Wild Chickens and Petty Tyrants: 108 Metaphors for Mindfulness*.

The alphabetized reflections contained herein are intended to inspire the integration of mindfulness into the fabric of daily life, and to encourage regular practice of mindfulness meditation. They can be read straight through or at random. I suggest you read the first entry on acceptance and then move where you like—on to the next or to whatever topic captures your interest. Read and reflect on one per day, and in a few months you may notice yourself living more intentionally, deliberately, and with greater ease. Each entry is an invitation to entertain, embrace, and embody a facet of mindfulness. Some entries contemplate Buddhist teachings that extend considerably beyond the practice of mindfulness as a means of managing stress, to the possibility of awakening itself.

Claiming the here and now is preferable to spiraling down into reactivity—being upset at being upset and missing out on the opportunity of this moment. I'm no stranger to that spiral. I'm right there with the rest of humanity, trying to live a happier, more meaningful life—trying to find a way beyond mere reactivity as some of my stories will reveal. Remembering to be mindful in every moment can be difficult to do. Yet the ideas in this book are not difficult to understand. They are straightforward and available to anyone at any time. Since you are reading this, I am pleased to know that this may be your time.

Arnie Kozak

Mindfulness A to Z

Acceptance

A is for *acceptance*.

I sat my first vipassana retreat in 1989. The first meditation retreat can be brutal on the body. I had my share of stiffness and soreness, especially in my knees. About seven days into the process I couldn't get comfortable no matter what position I struck. There was no escape from the pain unless I was willing to abandon the retreat—a thought I relished for a long while. So there I was, sitting with the agony, hour after hour, fighting against it, wishing it wasn't there. During one of the hour-long sittings I realized I had a choice: I could continue resisting the pain or I could try to accept it.

I chose acceptance. I turned my attention *toward* the sensations instead of away, which is where I instinctively wanted to go. After a week of practice, I had developed a level of concentration that allowed me to look precisely at my own bodily discomfort. My first approximation of that discomfort was that it was solid, intractable, difficult—like a railroad spike had been pounded into my knee. As I got closer to it with concentration, I noticed something else: oscillation, variation, and cessation. Within the discomfort there were moments of peace surrounded by moments of intensity. There was no "pain," only energy. The story of how awful it was dropped away, leaving only the bare experience of it. After that sitting, the tension in my muscles released; my body relaxed into the moment, and the rest of the retreat was free from that particular suffering.

When we are mindful, when we give our full attention to whatever is happening now, and can do so without the usual storytelling, pushing, pulling, and judgment, we arrive at acceptance. But it is rare that we give our full attention to what is happening now. We give partial attention; the rest of our attention is somewhere else. We are easily distracted. Our attention is always alighting some place other than here; we may think about what's for dinner, or review a past conversation. Wherever our attention is, it is not here, fully experiencing this present moment.

Thus, every moment of our existence presents us with the same basic choice that confronted me on the retreat. We can be present to what is happening, or we can fight against it. The tendency to resist is automatic, reflexive, and perhaps even compulsive. It may be relentless. Like a comfort-seeking missile, we may tweak, adjust, and modify every circumstance. Or, in the rare moments when things feel perfect, we may worry about losing the experience, and in these moments we are resisting the inevitable changing nature of things.

Acceptance is not acquiescence. We find ourselves in many situations that are not ideal. In some such situations reasonable action can be taken to change things. However, there are many situations in life where a simple act to change things is neither feasible nor possible. In such situations, acts of resistance become fruitless, and acceptance becomes a more meaningful option. When we resist, we are, in a sense, complaining about the situation. The complaint creates a boundary between oneself and the experience one is having at that moment. It takes energy to maintain that boundary. Our sense of "me" pushes against the reality of the situation and cries: "I don't want this."

We spend the moments of our lives pushing against what is so, wishing it were somehow different. Acceptance is a profound—perhaps the most profound—way of being in the world. It opens us to the raw, unadulterated experience of life in the moment. It is the only way to meet life as it is; everything else is fantasy, imagination, and hope. You can practice acceptance right here, right now. As you sit, feel the breath moving into your body. Give your full attention to the sensations of breathing without trying to change it in any way. Let go of thoughts about the future, the past, and elaborations of the present. Accept the simplicity of this moment, of the natural act of breathing. When your attention wanders from the act of breathing, don't let it perturb you. Accept that such wandering happens and simply bring the attention back to the breath.

It's a happy accident that the first entry of this book is acceptance. We could probably end the book here too. Acceptance is, in many ways, a synonym for mindfulness and the awakening it promises.

Adversity

I've torn the medial meniscus—the cartilage in my left knee. It's a vexing and debilitating injury, which takes me out of my usual active routines. I missed a month of golf in the fall and there was no snow-boarding or indoor golf for me that winter. This could have become a source of much anguish: "Poor me." But just because my knee hurts and the pain must be respected doesn't mean it must be worshipped. I can observe the injury-induced limits with a degree of equanimity— careful observation and interest that is not personalized. In other words, there is no "me" to feel sorry for.

Reality is what it is; I made an appointment with an orthopedic sur-geon. My mind could then relax; there was nothing to do but to take care of myself in the moment. Fretting about it and worrying about the larger shape of my life wouldn't help the situation. The injury may be healed with surgery—or it may not. The injury could leave an endur-ing stamp on my life. If that were the case, I would have to deal with new limitations, whatever they may be. As it turns out, the surgery is a success and I resume normal activities.

Things happen, things that we don't want to have happen—sickness, aging, death, and losses of every kind. It seems that we can see even little everyday setbacks, disappointments, or failures as things to be avoided at all cost. The fear of failure, of meeting with what we do not want, feeds our storytelling impulse and pushes us away from the reality of the moment.

Contemplating our biology can help us to understand why we are this way. Nature has provided us with mechanisms that help us to successfully navigate through a world filled with danger. Our natural emotions guide us: anger, fear, and shame keep us safe from potential harm; joy, pleasure, and interest support the long-term projects of survival and reproduction. Negative emotions are our threat-detection system. It's a straightforward system: approach things that feel good, withdraw from things that feel bad, ignore things that seem to be neither.

In contemporary culture, especially in the privileged cultures of the developed world, the survival-oriented function of negative emotion is largely obsolete. We can buy our food at supermarkets; we don't have to contend with predators; we have central air conditioning and heating systems. We still have to contend with social strife, but in an advantaged society, we don't have to worry about having our homes marauded by a rival clan of hunter-gatherers.

Because we live in a less threatening world, we have come to see threat-oriented emotions as bad. It's as simple as that—feeling unpleasant is bad. Our relationship to negative emotions can be seen by the way "necessities" like headache remedies, fabric softeners, and even prescription drugs are advertised. Such ads seem to suggest that we should never feel unpleasant, uncomfortable, or encumbered in any way. If the little aches and difficulties of daily life creep in, there is a product we can buy to ameliorate that unfortunate condition. The implicit message is that we should *always* feel pleasant, comfortable, and free from adversity. We've become afraid of our natural emotional life.

Adversity doesn't have to spoil a good mood so long as we can accept what is happening. We can retain a sanguine disposition if we can be interested in what is happening and not engage in storytelling about how the particular adverse occurrence is ruining our day. Adversity that is not life threatening or that does not lead to enduring harm is just an experience. It is an experience that we might even find interesting as it unfolds moment by moment, if we can just allow it to be there without preoccupation, without seeing it as an indictment against our lives. We may even look at big-ticket adversity items that do lead to harm as a teacher. It is possible to transform financial failure, cancer, or natural disasters into learning experiences when we can bring mindful attention to our lives even as such events unfold.

Anger

His Holiness the Dalai Lama has noted that it is hard to control oneself during an episode of anger. "Although one may know intellectually that anger is destructive, that one should not let oneself be swayed by the power of anger, that one must cultivate love toward others and so on, the chances of recalling this are very limited when engulfed in the heat of anger. In fact, thinking of love at that moment seems very impractical—it's farewell to love and compassion."

Our figures of speech suggest that anger is a force that must be discharged. We *lose our cool* and *blow our tops*. We *burn* with anger. These metaphors also seem to suggest that we are not entirely responsible for our anger—it's a force that happens to us, rather than something we choose. But anger, like all strong emotions, emerges from a confluence of natural forces and personal choices.

When we can notice the energy of anger arising in our bodies, choice becomes possible. Without that ability to notice, we just react like insects—stimulus and response. Noticing allows us to intervene with awareness. Awareness allows us to observe the sensations and energy that build up in our bodies. Noticing the breath shortening, growing quick and shallow, we recognize the onset of anger and can choose to change its expression. Instead of acting out like the Hulk, we might investigate the intense, embodied experience of anger, and through that investigation, exercise choice—a different way of being.

Anger may also be directed at oneself. At such times, it is just as disruptive, violent, and destructive as it is when directed elsewhere. We might get angry with ourselves for getting angry with someone else. We might get angry with ourselves when our attention wanders during meditation. We might get frustrated when our progress with meditation does not unfold according to preconceived plans. But as Lodro Rinzler, author of *The Buddha Walks Into a Bar*, cautions, "In twenty-six hundred years of meditation and teaching, no Buddhist master has ever said, 'You should just be a prick to yourself. That's how you create inner change.'" Anger can be harmful no matter where it is directed.

There are a few situations where anger is appropriate. Anger is natural in response to a truly threatening situation, but the vast majority of situations are not really threatening. Most of the situations in which anger typically arises only menace my idea of what *should* be happening in that moment. I am more vulnerable to my emotions, especially those in the anger family—anger, irritability, and frustration—when I don't practice mindfulness daily. With a modicum of practice I become capable of noticing the early warning signs of anger, which arise as bodily sensations. With continued practice I may even anticipate situations likely to provoke anger and move into them with an eye on my body, ready for the arrival of this potentially unskillful passion. If I notice its first stirrings, I may be able to circumvent the reaction entirely, thereby averting both the destructive social effects of expressing anger and its harmful internal effects, such as contributing to chronic stress.

Even with the best of intentions and a foundation of practice, anger may still arise in ways that are unhelpful. All is not lost, however, because mindfulness can be brought in after the fact to contain its ugly effects. One evening in the winter I came home to find the wood-stove cold when it should have been warm. I realized that I had left the flue open all day—a dangerous situation because that particular stove burned very hotly. Supernova hot. This was the third time that week I had left it open, although I was certain I had closed it that morning. I was chagrined, astonished, and indignant that I had dropped the ball again. The situation had exceeded what I could accept. My habitual reflex emerged—a near involuntarily efflux of anger. I yelled expletives aloud at myself.

After a brief meltdown, I sat down on my cushion, found my breath, and noted the tight sensations occupying my body. Awareness of the sensations helped to curtail any further anger. I had to check plaintive thoughts, not only about the open flue, but also about the mindlessness it represented. I sat with it all, acknowledged that it happened, inquired into the triggers of that particular moment, probed alternate possible responses should the situation arise again, and then settled back into the present moment. The anger gave way to a sense of peace; I shivered and lit a new fire.

Whatever our personal emotional tendencies may be, mindfulness can help us to be less angry with ourselves, others, and situations in our lives. Mindfulness can help us to become intimate with the energy of anger, and because of that familiarity we won't be blindsided by it. Instead, anger becomes information about our view of the current situation—feelings which, when recognized, can be a prompt indicating that we need to shift that view from one of resistance to one of acceptance.

Attention

"Hotel Renfrew? Looks more like a department store," I said to myself as I was walking around Montreal. "Maybe the hotel is on the upper floors." It turns out that the name of the establishment was "Holt Renfrew," and it's not a hotel at all (it is actually a high-end department store). I really didn't read the name, didn't give it my full attention. I assumed it was a hotel—fooled by the commonality of letters in "Holt" and "hotel" and because it was in a part of town that had a lot of hotels.

Misperceptions like this happen all the time. We can't process all of the information—the overwhelming amount of information—available in any moment. We select. And what we select depends on what's on our minds, what we've been exposed to recently, and myriad other factors. I was looking for a hotel near to Holt Renfrew, so that task biased my perception. Attention can be flimsy, fickle, and faint. It can be opportunistic and lazy. When I buy a new car, I start to notice that same model all around town. Those cars were there before; I just didn't have a reason to notice them.

It's hard for the untrained mind to sustain attention—in other words, to concentrate—without a compelling context. Even in compelling contexts, such as having sex, it may only devote a portion of itself to the experience. Try to focus on any object that you can see now; give it your full attention. Stop the exercise whenever you have a discursive thought about the object—an association, a memory, or an unrelated thought. Go ahead. Try it now.

For most of us the exercise will only last a few seconds. While we were all expected to pay attention in school, I've never met anyone who was shown how. Mindfulness is a way to train attention. Once we acknowledge that our attention is neglected, underdeveloped, and narrow, we can see the wisdom in training it to be more concentrated, robust, and responsive. We can move from living life on automatic pilot to giving our attention to the experiences that are happening now. Life becomes more vivid, rich, and intentional. These qualities help us to become more engaged with our lives, increasing our chances for happiness. When attention is superficial, the quality of life is likewise on the surface. When attention is deep, the quality of life will likewise go beyond the surface, revealing a world not otherwise appreciated—a world of perceptions, meanings, and revelations.

The late psychologist Julian Jaynes likened conscious attention to asking a flashlight in a dark room what the room looks like. Everywhere the flashlight is directed, the room appears illuminated. Likewise, we can't see all the moments of our lives when our conscious attention is dark, as they become when we move through the world lost in stories.

Conscious attention is a very small part of what our brains do—a sliver of a sliver. Most of what our brains do is unconscious, performed without explicit attention. This unconsciousness allows us to walk,

drive, and do most of what we do every day without having to th.
about it. The philosopher Alfred North Whitehead said, "Civilizatio.
advances by extending the number of important operations which we
can perform without thinking about them." While civilization may
advance, this automaticity can become a problem for individuals if it
is the prevailing, or only, mode of being in the world.

Attention is a skill, and as with all skills, it is a trainable one. While
attention is not a muscle, it responds to being exercised much as a
muscle does. It gets stronger, more flexible, and toned. The brain
regions devoted to attention grow thicker the more we exercise the
faculty. Mindfulness meditation is exercise for the mind that produces
mental fitness. We build attention by practicing the art of the gentle
return.

- Take a few minutes and try to focus on something like your
  breathing in this moment.
- Each time your attention moves away, gently bring it back.
- You'll notice the sensations are different now, and in a few
  moments attention will be off somewhere else again.
- Once more, catch your wandering attention and bring it
  back.

This practice exercises your attention "muscle." Returning is more
important than keeping your attention rigidly fixed. The more you
practice returning, the more fit your mind will become.

Attunement

We are social creatures to our core. We are born into a relationship—
the infant-caregiver bond. This connection directly affects the way our
brains develop, especially in areas devoted to how we see other people, the world, and ourselves. Those areas of the brain are integral for

managing stress and feelings such as fear. They are the areas of the brain responsible for social and emotional intelligence. If all goes well, we live in the world with engagement, ease, and happiness. If all does not go well—as is often the case—we may struggle with disconnection, anxiety, and discontent.

An infant's needs are changing second by second. To observe attunement in action researchers have videotaped mothers and their babies to examine how they interact frame-by-frame. When the interactions between babies and their mothers were slowed down in this way, researchers saw that the two were highly attuned to one another. Subtle cues from baby-to-mother and mother-to-baby directed the interaction. It's a subtle, intricate dance that requires attentiveness and skill on the part of the mother. She must subordinate her own needs to those of the child. And this is not just warmth, attentiveness, or nurturance, but well-timed, highly attuned warmth, attentiveness, and nurturance.

Brain researcher Dan Siegel has made the case that when we practice mindfulness meditation, we are engaging in self-attunement, like a mother (or father) attunes herself to her infant. Let's give it a try:

- With your attention, locate the breath moving in your body.
- Rest your attention on its ebb and flow.
- Attend to your body as a mother attends to her infant; treating it with gentle, caring regard.
- Don't try to control your breath; simply attend to it as a father holds his baby.
- Follow with interest the sensations and movements of your body as it breathes; meet it where it is, and enjoy simply observing the process of being alive.

When you practice in this way, you are engaging in self-attunement.

When we sit and observe our experience as it unfolds, moment-by-moment without judgment, storytelling, or commentary, we re-create an ideally attuned environment. We respond to our being, moment-by-moment, monitoring it with an attention, awareness, and warmth that come naturally from positive self-regard.

Seigel remarks that it is a lovely surprise that the areas of the brain affected by mindfulness meditation practice are the very same areas of the brain that undergo critical development during early infant attunement. The practice of mindfulness develops our sense of attunement with others, the world, and ourselves, allowing us to be in the world with greater ease.

Authenticity

Existential philosophers have long contended that a happy life stems from an authentic life. As a mindfulness-based psychotherapist, I feel it is very important not to pretend that I've gained complete mastery of mindfulness. I endeavor to be mindful, just as do the people I try to help. Sometimes my own endeavor is a struggle, as you will discover in some of the entries throughout this book. If I hid my imperfections, I'd be phony—inauthentic. To be authentic we must consider reality and our relationship to it.

But there's a hitch. What we know from centuries of philosophy, science, and, more recently, psychology is that our experience of reality is largely influenced by our own perception of it. To be sure, there is some kind of real world out there that we interact with all the time, but we also actively construct our experience of reality. Some of this constructedness is a hardware issue: we can only see what our eyes allow us to see and hear what our ears are capable of hearing. Some of this constructedness is a software issue: when we pay attention to an experience, our perceptions may be biased by what has happened to us, in terms of learning, trauma, and experience, either recently or in the remote past.

Our memories are influenced by our emotional states. They are more like paintings than photographs when it comes to accurate representations of objective reality. Under conditions of high emotional strain—especially in interpersonal situations—our painting-like memories may shift from being photorealistic to being abstract expressionist. Even a Hopper that depicts its scene "realistically" selects what to represent. But when a strong emotion like fear or anger arises, our perception may quickly distort the scene into a de Kooning—frenzied color and movement, with some sense of the original object, but deformed, disfigured, and twisted.

In order to be authentic, we must try to understand our psychological biases and how they affect our perception of the world and ourselves. We must develop an awareness of the gap that exists between our interpretation of things and the way they are in reality. We must be able to truthfully, honestly, and practically observe the influence of our biases. We must endeavor to know ourselves through our patterns of thought, our stories, and the emotions that these give rise to. It is downright impossible to be authentic without cultivating an awareness of the patterns of our minds. Mindfulness can be thought of as the practice of becoming intimate with the mind; it is a method that will help us to uncover these biases, conditionings, and predilections.

My boss for a part-time job that I have teaching at the university has a particular knack for triggering my emotions. We have had a couple of interactions that have really hooked me. Both times, I experienced him as authoritarian, paternalistic, and rigid. Each time, I felt indignant with a strong need to defend myself. The first instance led to a protracted and, at times, ugly email exchange that left me feeling alienated. The second instance arose, fortunately, while I was editing this manuscript, and I thought about how I could apply the principles of this entry to this situation. The emotions of this situation seemed big, and by stepping back and suspecting they might be biased, I was able to recognize that they were much bigger than the situation called for. This man really doesn't have any meaningful authority over me and I don't have to convince him that I am right. I realized that the energy for this exchange lived in my past relationship with my late father.

In the grand scheme of things, the issue was trivial and I could let it go. Before I let it go, I did draft an email response rebutting him point-by-point, but I let that email sit in my draft box. Like President Lincoln used to do with many of his letters, I did not send it. Sending the email would have been unskillful. If I felt a need to further pursue the issue it would have been more skillful to call or set up a meeting, since in person I have experienced him in a very different way. However, after my reflection, I no longer needed to prove anything. Insight into my own contribution to this affair deflated it and along with it my sense of self-importance.

To be genuine, we acknowledge our emotions, whether they are negative or positive. We can understand that emotions are a part of who we are, recognize where they come from, when they are useful and when they are not, and learn to manage them more effectively. We may struggle, stumble, and fall down every day, but if we are honest with ourselves about who we are, we will be able to pick ourselves up and try again. We may even learn to laugh at what once seemed intensely dramatic incidents of emotional outrage.

Aversion

I, like most everyone else, gravitate toward the things I like and feel repelled by the things that I don't. I am constantly pushed and pulled between these two tendencies. All that pushing and pulling can be exhausting and leads to anxiety. If I have what I want: "I might lose it!" If I don't have what I want: "I need to have it!" If I have what I don't want: "This is awful and it needs to change." And no matter what: "Things will never be exactly the way I want—in other words, perfect—therefore I can't be happy.

Why are we so afraid of imperfection? Why are we so motivated to avoid even the minutest inconvenience? If we think about it, it's not just big-ticket items like death and disease that bother us. It could be the temperature of the room, the size of the portion on our plate, or the balance of our bank account. It could be what other people say, think, or do. It could be our own thoughts, emotions, or bodily sensations. Aversion is a constant pressure and a major source of anguish. It is hard to be comfortable when we are always on guard against something happening that we don't want. No peace can emerge from that tension.

Aversion is part of our biological legacy. We need to avoid things that are potentially dangerous, whether it's predators or poisonous mushrooms. Aversion, which gives rise to negative emotions such as anger and fear, prepares us to fight or flee. Yet we find ourselves in a world where perceptions of threat occur even in the absence of any real threat. Instead of tigers hidden in the bush, we fear never living up to our expectations for ourselves. Our human capacity for imagination conspires with basic biological tendencies to create a matrix of anxiety. No place is safe when stalked by our own minds.

Despite our wish to be so, we cannot be comfortable all the time. We may pursue the perfectly imagined "good life," filled with everything we want and devoid of anything we don't, but we are unlikely ever to attain it. Even if we were lucky enough to attain some semblance of it, how could we ever expect it to last? If we don't expect to be comfortable, then we won't be so disappointed when we are uncomfortable. If we don't expect everything to go our way, then we won't be so disappointed when it doesn't. If we can be in the moment without expectations, there are no edges to press against and no place for aversion to take hold.

- Be mindful of the frequency of complaints in your vocabulary.
- Watch out for thoughts that begin with "I don't like . . ." and "I don't want . . ."
- When you notice that you are complaining, pause and redirect your attention to how that complaint shows up in your body such as tension or feeling ill-at-ease.
- Ask yourself what you gain from complaining about little annoyances.

- Let go of expectations and return your attention to the energy in your body.
- If the complaints are futile, pursue them less moving forward.

Mindfulness is a tool that we can use to recognize and undermine our tendency to complain. Rather than feeding our sense of aversion, we can use mindfulness to appreciate the moment without expectation.

Awakening

Buddha comes from the Pali word "buddh," meaning "to awaken." When Siddhartha had his insights under what is now known as the Bodhi tree, he told people that he had become Buddha—he had become an awakened one. His choice of the word implies that following his enlightenment he realized that he had previously been asleep.

As the traditional story goes, Siddhartha was a prince who lived a life of luxury, ease, and pleasure. His father, wanting to protect him from the world, sheltered him from the realities of sickness, old age, and death. Despite his perfect hedonistic existence, he still found something missing in his pampered life. Not until Siddhartha was nearly thirty years old did he, allegedly, see the marks of sickness, old age, and death. Now his gnawing sense that something was off became a full-blown existential crisis. At the age of twenty-nine, just after the birth of his son, he left his noble life to seek a way beyond suffering.

He practiced severe ascetic practices with forest-dwelling monks for seven years, becoming a virtuoso yogi, able to reach very high states of consciousness. Yet he always came down from those highs, right back into that unsatisfactory state—a state permeated by the sense that something was off. After nearly starving himself to death, he decided it was time to eat, take a bath, and find a new way to approach his goal. He sat down under a pipal or banyan fig tree and resolved not to get up until he had reached his aim and found a path to liberation.

The Buddha's novel and revolutionary insight was that our anguish arises from the activity of the mind. We further compound our misery by misapprehending the nature of things. Everything in life—the world, our experiences of it, and ourselves—is always changing, just as surely and unfailingly as we are always breathing, from the first moment of life to the very last. But that is not how it seems to us. Our world and our experiences all seem to be substantial, lasting, and real things. We do not see ourselves as a fleeting process but as a thing somehow standing outside of process. We mistake what is really a process for a thing. This is the source of suffering: a confused belief in the substantiality of ourselves.

Our ordinary state is akin to being asleep; we sleepwalk through life caught up in self-protective concerns, anxious about the gains and losses occurring in every moment, and largely inattentive to the world around us. When Siddhartha woke up he saw three things clearly:

1) I construct my anguish
2) Things are changing
3) There is no self standing outside the changing flow of experience

With these insights he was freed from anguish.

Awakening is perhaps the most accurate and useful way to understand what happened to Siddhartha. Waking up is commonplace. We do it every morning. In every moment, we have the opportunity to wake from sleepwalking through our lives. With every breath we have a chance to awaken into this very moment as long as we take this breath with full attention. After all, paying attention to the breath was the principal method Siddhartha used to achieve his awakening.

Inhale, exhale, awaken.

Bodhisattva

Bodhisattvas are those people who strive to become enlightened in order to benefit others. The bodhisattva is a compelling model that inspires one to follow a way toward awakening. When one takes the vows to become a bodhisattva, one vows to make efforts in the direction of enlightenment for the benefit of all sentient beings. The metaphor of the bodhisattva is one of selfless sacrifice. When a practitioner reaches enlightenment, she is freed from the cycle of samsara—the exigencies of living in the world—and does not have to take rebirth in a human or any other form. The bodhisattva, rather than entering some deathless, blissful realm, takes rebirth in order to help others in need, and continues to do so birth after birth. She could escape and chooses not too.

A secular take on the bodhisattvas would be to see them as an analogy for compassion in action, here and now. The image of the bodhisattva invites us to envision enlightenment as something we are always working toward, as a perpetual work-in-progress. The bodhisattva ideal envisions awakening as a process, not as a destination. We can't get there, unpack our bags, and settle into nirvana. In every moment, we can awaken, remain asleep, or fall down.

In some moments, we awaken to our lives as they are, and at other moments we get so caught up in painful stories that we cannot. We die to sleepwalking and are reborn into now whenever we remember our breath again, whenever we remember to touch our experience with awareness. Committing to being a bodhisattva helps me to remember. It gives me a context for my efforts and the inevitable struggles that accompany trying to live an awakened life.

The simplest step toward helping others is not to bring more anger, fear, and mindlessness into the world. Practicing mindfulness every day is key. When I am mindful, peaceful, and smiling, it has a medicinal effect on the people around me. Some years into my professional career I decided to bridge the gap from my personal meditation practice to begin teaching meditation in my psychotherapy practice. Since then, teaching mindfulness has become integral to what I do professionally. Now I continue and expand that work through writing. If you are starting to notice your breathing throughout the day and if you are returning your attention to your body from vexing stories, then I am helping you to awaken, if only a little bit at a time. At the same time, you are helping me to fulfill my bodhisattva vow.

Each time you embrace the welfare of others, you are following the bodhisattva path. Each moment you step out of self-preoccupation to pay attention to the world around you, an opportunity to help will present itself. The bodhisattva image is aspiration and inspiration, whether taken formally or informally.

Body Scan

It's four a.m. I am awake again, and not by choice. As I emerge from dreaming, my mind is fitful, my body tense. Tomorrow's to-do list (actually today's) besieges me in the early morning quiet. I need more rest. This is a good time to do the body scan meditation, or "beditation" as I like to call it in such situations.

The body scan is a staple of mindfulness practice. We begin by attending to the breath, noting bodily sensations as the belly rises and falls, and then move our awareness slowly through the rest of the body doing the same thing. It is a guided tour of the body meant to extend our mindful attention to every part of the body, especially to parts that we have been unaware of, where tension is often concealed.

A thorough body scan can last up to forty-five minutes. Carefully working through the body gives you plenty of time to explore what is going on in there. During the body scan, investigate the physical sensations of the body as a researcher would investigate phenomena of interest. Approach the body, its movements, its tension with curiosity, as a scientist would approach something newly discovered. Be objective, interested, and descriptive. Ask yourself, "What are the findings?" Ask yourself, "What do I observe?" Good scientists are not for or against what they find; just the facts please.

Because stress lives largely in the body, the body scan is an integral practice for working with stress. And because emotions live in the body, the development of emotional intelligence also requires an awareness of what is happening in the body at any given moment. Body scanning was one of the practices that the Buddha relied on in his efforts to awaken, because it helps to cultivate awareness of the insubstantiality of ourselves and the evanescence of the body.

One of the qualities that the Buddha was known for during his life was having an exceedingly serene bodily comportment and a measured, natural gait. The body scan allows us to inhabit our bodies and to cultivate the type of bodily mindfulness reflected in the placid physicality of the Buddha. The body scan allows us to recruit the body as a grounded way of being in the world.

- Begin by bringing your attention to your breathing.
- Allow the breath to be natural; simply follow its movement.
- Pay attention to the physical sensations that arise as you breathe:
  - any tingling at the tip of the nose
  - the movement of moist air through the nostrils and mouth
  - the rise and fall of the belly as the breath passes the diaphragm.
- Attend to sensations both on the surface of the body and

within it as you breathe; try to attend to both obvious and subtle sensations.

- Begin to systematically move your attention throughout the body.
- Don't get hung up if you don't feel anything much in a particular part of the body. This is normal. The body is always changing; perhaps tomorrow there will be something to notice there. With practice you will begin to notice a great deal more of your body.
- Beginning with the toes of the left foot, explore the entire left leg up to the pelvis, followed by the right.
- Then move through the pelvic region, from the lower end of the torso to the upper, noting sensations in the abdomen, chest, and back.
- As the mind attends to the torso, breathing will again become the focus.
- Explore the arms, moving downward from the shoulders all the way to the tips of the fingers, noting the joints as attention passes through them.
- Lastly, investigate the head, attending to tension held in the neck, ears, and face.
- Once all the body parts have been examined, sweep the body as a whole, from the top of the head to the tips of the toes and fingers.

The sweep can be done quickly or slowly, according to preference. As an alternative to a systematic investigation of the entire body, you can ground your attention in the breath and then move it wherever sensations are most prominent. I recommend beginning with the systematic sweep, so no parts of the body are overlooked.

I've found the body scan to be a potent tool for treating insomnia. Students are sometimes instructed to do the body scan practice lying down. Since the body scan can be done while lying down, it can be practiced when one has trouble sleeping, and it can be an especially helpful remedy for waking in the middle of the night. The simple process of attending to the body distracts us from the worrisome and arousing stories that might be keeping us awake, allowing us to fall restfully to sleep. The practice can be repeated if we wake again. You may not fall asleep, but you are bound to get the restfulness that comes from the practice.

Boredom

Fritz Perls, the founder of Gestalt therapy, said, "If you are bored, you're not paying attention." This axiom could be a manifesto for mindfulness. By paying attention to what is happening we can generate interest, curiosity, and even fascination with the most mundane experiences of life.

Attention is a scarce resource. Since the world can be a threatening place and survival requires effort, cunning, and luck, our ancestors would have been well served by turning their attention away from things that weren't novel. Novelty indicated the potential for danger (that noise may be a tiger lurking in the grass) or for opportunity (that variation in the landscape may be a sign of water). So as efficient creatures we have evolved to look for novelty and to grow uncomfortable when we cannot find it.

But today, novelty and boredom occur in strikingly different contexts than they did for our ancient ancestors. Our survival no longer hangs on our ability to detect novelty in our environments. In the absence of real-world demands that motivated an attention that skips from thing to thing, we feel antsy. The craving for excitement can be temporarily sated by information, gaming, and entertainment, but in the end the constant barrage of novelties has exacerbated our boredom, rather than causing us to become more engaged. As attention spans decrease, the potential for boredom increases.

Boredom is but one of the many stories we tell ourselves. It's a story in which we are the stars. "*I* am bored." The story of boredom is one of entitlement: we should always be entertained, thrilled, and delighted, and not a moment of our lives should go by that is not fresh, exciting, and memorable. Or, as is often the case, not a moment should go by that isn't wasted; that is not in the service of something on our to-do list. As with most of the problems that storytelling can bring, boredom can also be remedied by attending to the breath.

Breathing usually seems quite boring—repetitive, commonplace, and irrelevant. But when we pay close enough attention, breathing can be fascinating. Our breath is always changing, subtly, unnoticed there beneath every experience. The never-ending ebb and flow of the breath is what sustains this life. It is a simple yet powerful bodily function that carries itself forward without needing to be impelled or directed in any way. Like waves rolling one after the other onto a beach, each breath, while mundane, repetitive, and cyclical, has a beauty that one only comes to appreciate after closely observing it.

We spend a lot of time waiting. While we await the arrival of a train, bus, or plane, we can drop into our bodies and attend to our breathing. Instead of flipping through magazines, surfing the web on our phones, or looking for some way to hurry past the moment, we might choose instead to sit and observe our breath. Why not treat unforeseen, and otherwise boring, gaps in the daily schedule as opportunities to relax and attend to the moment—to sit at the shore of our minds and watch the waves of each breath roll in and out? Facebook will still be there when the bus comes 'round.

Breath

I sit attending to the process of breathing. The air passes across the edges of each nostril, moves through the moist recesses of my mouth on its way to my throat. Lungs expand. The chest does not rise. The air instead fills the belly. Each inhale draws new vitality into this body. Each exhale disposes of whatever this body did not need—an efficient recycling of natural elements. The vitality of breathing overflows into arms, to the tips of fingers, and down through the legs to the toes. Each breath is quickly dispersed all throughout the body by a few beats of the heart. Where does the breath end and the body begin? I *am* breathing: whole, connected, and spacious.

Many objects of focus are suitable for mindfulness meditation—a candle flame, sounds such as a mantra, or some aspect of the natural world. The breath, however, offers many advantages over other objects of focus. Breathing always happens. (If it isn't happening, then meditation is the least of your problems!) Breathing happens in the body and is therefore always with us wherever we are. Breathing requires no effort, no recollection, no training. You are already doing it now. The quality of breathing mirrors our emotional states. When we are emotionally excited the breath becomes frenetic, and when relaxed, slow and smooth. The quality of breathing can likewise influence how we feel. Breathe rapidly and we begin to feel panicky; breathe deeply and slowly and we begin to feel tranquil.

Because breathing shares such an intimate connection with our feelings, it makes sense for those of us interested in cultivating emotional intelligence to pay attention to it. Doing so gives us the opportunity to remain in touch with our emotional states even as they unfold. Placing the attention on the breath is like keeping your finger on the pulse of your emotional life. The more you cultivate awareness of your emotions by watching the breath, the greater will be the opportunity to intervene when emotion begins to overwhelm you.

Attending to the breath is simple. But don't let its simplicity fool you. It is also a very profound practice, when consistently cultivated. It can lead all the way to spiritual awakening. Meditation on the breath is one of the foundational practices that the Buddha taught, and it remains a core practice of all Buddhist traditions because of its simplicity and the advantage of its object of focus.

- Begin by noticing your breathing.
- Allow the breath to be natural.
- Don't attempt to breathe in any special way.

- Simply observe the breath, as it is, whether slow or fast, coarse or refined, shallow or deep.
- After doing this for a few moments, you may notice that your attention has wandered away from the breath. It is quite common for the mind to become distracted with dreams about the future, reflection on the past, or elaboration of the present. If you notice such distraction, without judgment or recrimination against yourself, simply redirect your attention to the physical sensation of the breath as it moves through the body.
- Repeat this process each time distraction occurs.

Everyone's attention wanders from the breath. Mine does all the time, and I've been meditating for thirty years. The fact that attention sometimes wanders should not be surprising. This in itself is not a sign that something is wrong. Ours is a practice of learning to notice distraction when it happens. See if you can consistently return your attention to the physical sensations of the breath, without judging the quality of your mind. The object of breathing meditation is not to keep attention from moving away from the breath but to bring it back whenever it does. We are practicing the art of returning—the gentle return—rather than the art of staying put.

Buddha

Buddha was a person who lived in ancient India. But buddha is also a name given to the capacity each of us has for awakening. In the latter sense, both you and I are buddha, but this does not necessarily have to have anything to do with Buddhism. The idea of buddha as a living being's capacity to find peace is more a fundamental vision of the nature of life than a statement of institutional doctrine. "All beings seek happiness. None wish to suffer." Such natural tendencies can be attributed to our "buddha" nature.

The Buddha was not a Buddhist, any more than Jesus was a Christian. The Buddha likely did not see himself as a divine figure or in possession of special powers, despite the fact that later generations have come to see him that way. Rather, the core teachings of his faith suggest that he saw himself as a pioneer—someone who was forging a path that people would be able to follow on their own. He did sometimes compare himself with a physician and his teaching with medicine. The system, which he developed over his forty-five-year career as a teacher, was aimed at healing the suffering that afflicted humanity.

The first teaching he gave following his awakening, which has become the cornerstone of all Buddhist wisdom, was the teaching of what are called the Four Noble Truths. Buddha presented the four truths as if he were a doctor diagnosing and treating an illness. The first noble truth constituted his diagnosis—*dukkha* (i.e., there is suffering, stress, misery, anguish, dissatisfaction). Not only do we suffer, but we unwittingly compound our misery, and we are oblivious to the liberation that waits in the unfurling of every breath. The second noble truth provided the etiology of the illness: we are anguished because we are misguided about reality, because we cling to things that are changing as if they were not, and we overestimate the substantiality of our selves. The third noble truth delivered the prognosis: the outlook is optimistic; the condition is treatable. Because the nature of our illness is essentially one of mental habits, it is possible to remedy all of the mental activities that lead to suffering, anguish, and misery. The fourth noble truth is his prescription, the medicine that will heal the illness— cultivation of wisdom, ethical behavior, and meditation (known as the Noble Eightfold Path).

It is not unreasonable to think of the Four Noble Truths *as* the Buddha in both of the above senses. Not only do they represent the legacy and primary teaching of the person of the Buddha, they also represent a concrete expression of our natural inclination to seek peace.

The Buddha chose a monastic path, living his life as a mendicant in dependence on the charity of kings and peasants alike. Surely in those early days, the followers of the Buddha saw him as the man that he was—awakened, yet mortal. His image, however, has grown more and more godlike over the millennia. The myth of Buddha has over-shadowed the idea of buddha as our own nature, available to us right now. The awakening that waits within us may seem distant, almost unattainable, but it is available to us in this very moment. We touch it briefly when we practice mindfulness. If the Buddha could traverse the path, we can traverse it, too. *Everyone* can walk the path of a buddha.

Buddhism

"Are you Buddhist?" It is a question that I am often asked. Many assume that I am. When I tell people that I am not, they are surprised, especially because I have been practicing Buddhist-style meditation for over twenty-five years and recently wrote the second edition of *The Everything Buddhism Book*. "Some of my best friends are Buddhists," I would joke, "but I am not." I prefer to say that I am a "Buddhist without beliefs," to borrow the title of Stephen Batchelor's bestselling book. Buddhism is one of the world's great religions, and one that I deeply respect. Yet, like all religions, it can be prescientific and super-stitious. Much of what we think of as Buddhism may not even be what the Buddha actually taught and likely has only a distant connection to the historical Buddha. Authors like Batchelor, Andrew Olendzki, Mu Soeng, John Peacock, and other emerging voices of secular Buddhism argue that we might also understand the teachings of the Buddha within the context of the natural world, without recourse to metaphys-ical claims. If I had to be a Buddhist, I would be a secular Buddhist.

In some of the teachings that have been passed down, the Buddha seems to condemn metaphysical speculation. He likens human pre-occupation with metaphysical claims to the case of a person who has been shot with an arrow asking of what sort of wood the arrow was made, who made it, and how it came to be lodged in his body, instead of seeking the means to immediately remove it and treat the wound. We, like the wounded man, may become preoccupied with searching for answers to the unknowable while the basic condition of our suffering goes unchanged. If I am to be a Buddhist, I would be the type interested in the immediate relief of suffering, in this very moment, rather than in speculating about the nature of time, space, and the divinity of the Buddha. It would be better to just pull the arrow of suffering out.

While mindfulness meditation is a staple of Buddhist tradition, it is not necessarily "Buddhist." Breathing and attention are faculties that all humans possess. The Buddha merely worked skillfully with the conditions in which we find ourselves to fashion a method for treating the suffering that plagues us. We need not be initiated into any religious cult, nor take on belief in some metaphysics to rest our attention astride the breath. The cultivation of mindfulness is available to all of us, regardless of what we believe. In this sense mindfulness can be thought of as secular. It's about our experience right now, in the immediacy of each passing moment of our lives. It does not require any belief, -ism, or doctrine, only our own awareness. It is as natural—and universal—as the air we breathe.

Choice

Choice is available to us in every moment. The capacity to choose, born of awareness, is one of our most precious human capacities, and yet we often squander it. We make a lot of bad choices because we have difficulty containing our impulses. So we not only want to make choices, we want to make good choices. Mindfulness helps us to make good choices by giving us the time and sense of space within which to make them. Better choices follow better self-awareness.

I like to find my breath early in the morning. If it's not during formal practice, then I locate it while drinking coffee. Sitting and breathing, I have the opportunity to be aware that I am alive and that the day waits. It is in this space, connected to breathing, that I can make choices about how I'd like my life to unfold. Of course, our way of making choices is influenced by internal and external factors. There are personality-based factors that determine how easy or difficult it will be for us to make good choices. Our personality determines how sticky thoughts are, how much we ruminate and worry. Some of us have to work harder at it than others. I know I do.

I take comfort in Bhante Gunaratana's description of the mind in *Mindfulness in Plain English*, where he says, "You will come face to face with the sudden and shocking realization that you are completely crazy. Your mind is a shrieking, gibbering madhouse on wheels barreling pell-mell down the hill, utterly out of control and helpless. No problem. You are no crazier than you were yesterday. It has always been this way, and you just never noticed."

Automatic pilot cuts us off from the world around us. We can do most anything without conscious attention—walking, driving, eating, personal hygiene, etc. Attention is often somewhere else—in the future, the past, or lost in opinions about the activity of the moment. Mindfulness provides the opportunity to live in a deliberate fashion, to live life on purpose, with intention, and guided by meaning. Cultivating awareness helps us to render visible the invisible forces that push us along, to turn happenstance into the opportunity to choose. Mindfulness creates the space wherein we can live proactively instead of reactively.

By choosing to live intentionally, the quiet space opened by practice can be used to direct the arc of our lives. "How do I want to use my time and energy today? What do I want to accomplish in my life? How do I want to be?" If we don't set our own intentions, the people and situations around us will set them for us. One important choice we confront every day is whether to practice meditation. What will you choose today? If you sit, try being deliberate after you meditate. Take a few moments at the close of your practice to set your intention for how you'd like the rest of the day to unfold. Take advantage of your ability to choose.

Commentary

I am standing on top of an overlook in the foothills of the Green Mountains in the late afternoon. I can see a 180-degree vista to the West that features the Adirondacks, tinged in pink, as the sun gets ready to set. Vermont's famous Camel's Hump sits majestically to the south. The ground is covered in fresh snow. My mind, however, is not awed by this experience, at least not consistently so. I want to get some pictures of this, but I have forgotten my phone and thus have no camera. My mind complains about that, falling into the trap of wanting something it cannot have. I compare this particular view to the ones I've seen on other recent hikes up this spot. I think about my forthcoming dinner guests and what I need to do to prepare dinner. I tell myself how wonderful this is, how lucky I am to live here, and how beautiful the mountains are. Yet these are words, not the experience of it. Occasionally, though, I redirect my thoughts from this running commentary to the experience itself. As the words drop away, I have a different experience of the scene—one that is captured by my body instead of a camera.

The scene on the mountain is not unusual. Our lives are almost always accompanied by the running commentary track. Our minds are continually spinning out opinions about everything as it happens. Often the mind will wander into fantasy, weaving detailed stories about things that could happen, might have happened, and even about things that are unlikely to ever happen. Most of the time, even though such thoughts may be tied to the present moment, they obscure or muffle our *experience* of it. The running commentary is so pervasive and ever-present that we typically do not notice it at all. It fades into the background, part of the warp and woof of our daily lives. If we slow down and pay attention, however, the commentary can be heard, clear as day, as I did in the scene above.

Commentary creates incessant distraction from the experience of things as they are. Much of the time the commentary is a "color commentary," judging, valuing, or needlessly embellishing the experience at hand. "I like this" or "I don't like this," it says. Or it simply strings along a mindless series of associations, one after the other, without much rhyme or reason, until one can't recall how one reached the point of thinking one's thoughts. Tangled up in commentary, our minds are caught in a constant push and pull against experience. Rather than seeing things for what they are, we're always thinking how they could be better, or how this moment compares with some other, or we fail to see things at all, distracted by the proliferation of unassociated mental chatter.

If we are mindful, it is possible to turn off the commentary and instead to fully experience what is happening now. We need simply recognize when our attention has wandered from the moment at hand to the commentary on it, and then choose to redirect our attention back to the experience actually unfolding in a given moment. One of the fruits of consistent practice of mindfulness is the ability to recognize when we have become distracted by commentary, even as we move through our lives away from the meditation cushion. My practice did not avert the running commentary on top of the hill but it did give me the chance to recover my attention, at least in moments. Importantly, I didn't beat myself up for the commentary. I know it is a strong feature of the mind. Noticing the presence of commentary in our daily lives can also help us to recognize it in our practice of mindfulness. The reprimand, reproach, and castigation that sometimes appear when we find we've lost our focus on the breath are just other types of commentary. See if you can note commentary and leave it behind.

Compassion

My hulking Rhodesian ridgeback, Ruki, was in pain. His condition was getting progressively worse. We tried one medication, then another. Each worked for a few days, but then the pain broke through. Eventually the only option left was morphine, but dogs cannot take morphine by mouth. The drug was compounded into a special paste, which I rubbed inside his huge floppy ears.

For a few days he no longer winced in pain when he moved, though his gait was badly hobbled. Ruki no longer accompanied me to the office or meditation studio, as he used to. When I came home from work on a Friday, he was too weak to get up from the floor to greet me. He could not move his hind legs—at all. The pain had returned. He whimpered with each exhalation.

That night I slept on the floor next to him, rubbing morphine into his ears on the hour, using as much medicine that night as in the previous week. I could feel his anguish. He spoke with his eyes what he could not speak with words. We huddled together through the night, waiting for morning and the one-way trip to the vet's office. During those hours, I set aside my own distress. My job was to breathe with Ruki. There is no room to introduce one's stories into such situations. I had to open myself wholly to him, to quietly accompany him through the worst of it, to let him know that he wasn't feeling it alone.

Compassion unfolds out of the simple act of paying attention to another. Compassion means "to suffer with," and it can be distinguished from sympathy, which means "to feel with." Sympathy, while not an ignoble impulse, implies distance between oneself and the suffering of others; compassion includes a desire to alleviate the suffering of the other. When we feel sympathy, we relate to the narrative of the suffering of others, as if we were spectators—somewhat involved, but safely removed from it. Compassion is similar to sympathy, but with openness afforded by lack of storytelling.

The practice of compassion begins with a conscious silencing of thoughts of "I" and "mine," which tend to turn the experience of other's suffering into stories about ourselves. Just as we learn to relate to ourselves without judgment and to return attention to the breath with the practice of mindfulness, we learn to attend to others unconditionally, without injecting our own color commentary into the situation, and to return our attention to others when practicing compassion. Compassion builds on the nonjudgmentalism that we cultivate with mindfulness, extending to others the regard with which we learn to treat ourselves.

While compassion allows us to be open and unconditionally available to others, the element of mindfulness allows us not to become overinvolved with narratives about the suffering of others. Compassion is a willingness to look at another human being, animal, or situation without filters or preconditions, to see things clearly as they are. The compassionate view is generous with regard to others. It says, "I am willing to dismantle the wall of stories that I naturally construct to defend myself against identifying with your painful experience. I am willing to open to you as you are, even as you suffer."

Even our compassion can be mindful. When we drop our guard and accept the pain of others with the emotional clarity, spaciousness, and stillness that come with the practice of mindfulness, we become capable of caring for others without ourselves being emotionally overwhelmed.

Concentration

Over the six-month long Vermont winters, the roads can get icy. Driving on these slick surfaces compels a mindful approach. One New Year's Eve, following an end-of-the-year celebration at a rural Zen center, I had to make my way home just after a shower of freezing rain had fallen. After leaving the center I encountered a tow truck operator rescuing a car that had gotten stuck nearby. He warned me that all the roads in the area were coated with black ice. Nevertheless, I had to get myself and my passenger, a good Dharma friend, home.

The conditions demanded that I keep my attention unwaveringly riveted to the road and to any subtle changes in the vehicle's interaction with it. There was no room for the distraction by fretful inner commentary. I also couldn't afford to be tense. The commentarial mind can be very insistent, particularly so in dangerous situations. In order to prevent any distracting intrusion by this mind, I marshaled my concentration, fixing it squarely on the road *and* on setting my passenger at ease with intermittent jokes about our harrowing situation. This kept me relaxed and attentive and, most importantly, prevented any self-conscious tension. The car stayed on the road.

Concentration comes easily if the situation is compelling enough. Driving on the icy road, my mind easily became concentrated, my senses heightened. It's harder to maintain concentration in situations that are not particularly compelling, which is the case in most moments of our mundane lives. Unless some compelling condition emerges as we shower, dress, walk, drive, or eat, we are quite capable of completing all daily tasks with hardly any concentration at all. It's as if we are on automatic pilot for much of our day.

Right Concentration is a part of the Buddha's Noble Eightfold Path. Concentration is not an end in itself, but it is instrumental on the path to awakening. Concentration on the breath helps to quiet the mind and establish a foundation of mental stability upon which one might successfully investigate the nature of experience. Once we have developed the skill of concentration, of sustaining attention, we can afford to leave off single-pointed concentration on the breath and begin examining the nature and quality of sensations and emotions as they arise within the body during meditation.

The practice of analyzing our experience as it unfolds is called *vipassana* or insight meditation. Being able to maintain our awareness of the arising, oscillation, and dissolution of thoughts, emotions, images, and sensations can lead to insight into the fleeting nature of the moment. Insight into the nature of experience is said to be the remedy for suffering, and the successful practice of insight meditation is only possible when grounded by steadfast concentration.

We tend to think of concentration as a laser-like focus on a single thing. We can also think of concentration as paying sustained attention to whatever is most *relevant* in a given moment. Sometimes maintaining sustained attention on only that which is relevant in an environment requires a concentration that is highly focused, and at other times it requires a concentration that is more broadly distributed, capable of being spread widely across distinct dimensions of experience. Driving my car home over rural ice-covered roads required a broadly distributed concentration, for example. I had to maintain my focus on the road, the car's interaction with it, and my passenger's uneasiness with the situation all at once!

Training in mindfulness includes both aspects of concentration. At the beginning, we learn to focus our attention very narrowly on the breath, on just the very tip of the nose or on the breath as it enters the nose, flows into the lungs, down to the diaphragm and back out. As our skill develops, we learn to attend to multiple dimensions of the breath, including thoughts and feelings that arise in association with the practice. The flourishing of mindfulness—noticing that attention has strayed from its object and bringing it back—produces concentration—sustained attention on the object at hand. Concentration is not a rigid imposition of attention; rather it is the expression of a robust mindfulness.

Containment

As I write this entry, I've left my seat, again. An impulse arose and I acted upon it, finding myself walking into the kitchen looking for something to eat. I was already away from my computer before I realized what was happening. I didn't make a conscious choice to get up; it seemed like I was imperceptibly compelled from within to move from my spot. This happens more than I would like. I find, however, that if I bring a bit of mindfulness to my work at the computer, I am much more capable of noticing such impulses as they arise and am able to contain them. One of the benefits of developing the skill of mindfulness is greater containment of unconscious impulses.

As a species we may be *homo sapiens*, "thinking man," but as organisms we are challenged with a great number of natural biological impulses that occur with little or no thought behind them. Impulses to seek food, drink, make meaningful social bonds, and reproduce serve biological imperatives related to survival. Impulses in search of a higher quality of life, replete with the resources for survival, an ideal sexual and life-partner, and fully decked-out territory to call one's own, are fed back to us culturally. The convergence of potent biological impulses with powerful cultural messages about what a desirable life entails creates the potential for impulses ballooning into obsessions. Without putting much thought into it, we find that we just cannot be satisfied while lacking what we perceive to be requisites of "the good life," whether it is a flat screen television or a family.

Containment is the mindfulness-related skill of managing impulses so that they don't become obsessions or destructive behaviors. Mindfulness can be used to contain and manage impulses by creating a space between, for instance, the urge to seek something to snack on and abandoning my work at the computer. As we grow accustomed to being mindful, our attention to mental events naturally improves and we develop greater awareness of them as they motivate our actions. Awareness of mental events prior to the onset of action is experienced as a "gap"—a precious pause where choice can occur.

The term "containment" does not mean suppression of impulses. Suppression is a very hardline approach to behavior, which seeks to judge, deny, squelch, or ignore impulses. Containment means to use the gap opened up by mindful awareness between impulses and reactions to them to consciously choose one's course of action. The gap opened up by mindfulness can be used as a judgment-free space in which to relate to our natural impulses, and to explore them with interest and positive regard. The exploration of impulses, of whether they represent substantial pressing needs or habitual patterns of empty self-gratification, is the beginning of the process of changing habitual behavior patterns.

Learning to thoughtfully relate to impulses and developing the ability to choose whether to react to them or not has immediate benefits in terms of containing impulsive distractions as one concentrates on a task at hand—typing a manuscript at the computer, for example. And in the long run the practice of containment enables choice to intervene even between very strong, sudden emotional impulses and potentially explosive reactions to them, sparing oneself and others from the negative experience of ugly outbursts.

Only automatic, unconscious, and habitual emotions are able to compel rash behavior. The skill of containment allows us to act with

emotional intelligence. It is also a good example of how even inci-
dental skills developed through the practice of mindfulness can have
beneficial effects in our daily lives, both personally and socially.

The next time an impulse arises for you, see if you can observe it
with interest. Notice how it occupies your body and compels action. If
you are watching closely enough, you may be able to contain it before
it translates into behavior. Or, as is often the case, as the urge is set in
motion, you can catch it at the outset and make your choice then. I
often catch myself in the act of doing something that I did not intend to
do. These are perfect little moments for practice. In a sense, I choose
to make myself bigger than the energy that is driving the behavior. This
way I contain it with awareness.

Crasping

During his awakening, the Buddha discerned the sequence of events
that lead to all suffering. Buddha said that, from among the various
factors that lead to suffering, desire is the driving force that propels
us toward unhappiness. Of course, it is natural to have desires. There
is nothing innately wrong with wanting something or seeking comfort. As with many impulses, desire only becomes problematic when
embellished by storytelling. Simple desires become a source of anxiety
when our sense of well-being becomes dependent on the "need" to
have things a certain way. Desire exacerbated by anxiety and perceived
need becomes craving, and craving exacerbated by the discomfort of
not getting what one wants becomes grasping as we seek to fix the situation. Since these two almost always occur together, I have taken to
referring to them by the more economical term "crasping."

Often the things that we convince ourselves "need" to be different
for us to feel happy or comfortable are in reality not so important.
Many times they are simply those things that remind us in a visceral
way that we are living human beings—the temperature of the room,

the emptiness or fullness of our bellies, itches, aches, and pains in the body. Sometimes little reminders of our human condition are blown out of proportion by the storytelling mind, which strings us along with the idea that we'd be happy "if only . . ." Crasping happens when we get so bound up in what we think we need in order to be happy that we just can't feel comfortable until those "needs" are met.

I got my first Macintosh computer in 1987, a Mac SE—one of the first modular computers. When I got to grad school I became frustrated with its small black and white screen and its lumbering processing capacity. I started to crave a better model, the next step up—the Macintosh LCII, which had a big color monitor and processing speeds orders of magnitude better than the SE. Sufficiently motivated by the dissatisfaction bred by craving and grasping after the new model, I successfully obtained one, spending money I probably shouldn't have spent.

I was satisfied for a brief moment. Unfortunately, about a month after I bought the LCII, the LCIII was released. I may as well have been in hell. My recently won happiness vanished—I wanted the faster, newer model, and was angry, crestfallen, and frustrated that I ended up with the one I had. Of course, there was nothing truly unsatisfactory about the one I had. Craving and grasping had made it into a problem.

The question we should ask ourselves in the face of the fear of missing out is "Can we just let go?" By "letting go" I don't mean to suggest some stoic renunciation, but to approach our sense of crasping with a bit of detachment. Instead, we bring interest to what is going on in the moment. "This thing is happening now. What does it look like? What does it feel like? How is it changing moment by moment?" Interest begins to break the bonds of crasping.

This interest is the entry point to equanimity, from the Pali term *upekkha*—literally there in the middle of things. "There in the middle of things" we are not pushing it away, not pulling it toward us, holding on for dear life. Interest is the entry point for mindfulness. We can give whatever is happening our full attention and this attention can be infused with not just attentiveness but a host of other qualities, including equanimity. Instead of being closed, we can be open to the experience, giving ourselves degrees of freedom impossible to have when we react with crasping.

If we do this long enough, wisdom may just arise. We may understand at an intuitive level that it is simply easier to be in the world without this constant crasping. We may just realize that our energy is better spent enjoying things as they are than lamenting that they are not different.

In any given moment, try to make your best guess as to what course of action is going to lead to the best results. You won't get it right every time, yet through the habit of mindfulness, these guesses will bias things in the favorable direction. Anxiety permeates the crasping. "Will I get what I want? What happens if I don't get what I want? "What happens if I lose what I have? How can I be okay?" You can let go of these thoughts or counter them with other, more productive thoughts, such as "I am okay whether I get what I want or not." "My happiness does not depend on my always getting what I want." Without this constant anxiety you will be happier in the world, more content.

Creativity

The sculptor Henry Moore said, "If I set out to sculpt a standing man and it becomes a lying woman, I know I am making art." *Being* in the world is spontaneous with unexpected outcomes. When the mind clings to certainty, being is inhibited. Creativity gives us the opportunity to be surprised. Mindfulness opens us to the possibility of living in the world creatively—life becomes imaginative, each moment an act of creation coming into being. We never quite know what is going to happen next. If we are open to possibility, we may start out with one idea—a standing man—and wind up with another—a lying woman.

Every moment can be an inspired act, provided we are paying attention. You don't necessarily have to produce works of art; your life itself becomes the creative act. But often we don't pay enough attention to the singularity of each experience. We take shortcuts. It's efficient to put things into categories based upon similarity. It is functional to overlook minor distinctions. The avant-garde musician John Cage suggested looking at three "identical" bottles of Coca-Cola arranged in a row. While the bottles are functionally indistinguishable, perceptually they are unique. Light reflects differently and the image of each bottle hits the retina of our eye differently. The experience of each one is unique. An artist looks at the world in this way—looking for the minor distinctions instead of the major themes of similarity.

This shift in perceptual emphasis may not be natural for us to do; it may require practice to overcome the mind's tendency to categorize by sameness. The mind relies upon metaphor to move through the world. *This* is similar to *that*, so I will use *that* to understand *this*. *This* experience is similar in structure to *that* experience, so I don't have to pay attention to the singularity of *this* experience; I can process *this* (and more efficiently so) based on my past experience with *that* other thing. Art requires us to overcome this metaphorical habit to see the world in its phenomenological suchness.

I am sitting in a vast space in a contemporary art museum. The windows are six stories high and the sun is shining in, reflecting off a skyscraper beyond the windows. I have never been in this space before, yet when I saw the chairs arranged around a coffee table I knew that I could sit in them. My brain has a category for chairs. Further still, my brain has a category for these particular chairs—Mies van der Rohe Barcelona chairs, to be exact. This recognition pleases me. Now that I am situated in these objects—that is, sitting on one of the chairs—I have an opportunity. I can stay at the level of the familiar (the categorical) or I can let my attention sink into the present moment to appreciate what is here beyond the surface similarity—the vastness of this space, the way these chairs actually feel, the dancing of the afternoon light, the scope of the art, and the people moving through the space. I feel at home here. I feel my existence coming into being, and if I don't try to micromanage this experience, bliss follows closely behind. As soon as I co-opt it with a sense of self-referenced story, that ecstasy becomes shy. In the next moment, I return to the perception of the space, feel the enormity of this room, and smile once again.

I leave this vast room to explore other parts of the museum. I viewed this room once again from an open balcony on the upper floors. The seating arrangement once there was gone—moved for some other function that would happen in this space. This transition is a reminder of the dream-like quality of existence—always changing; impermanent.

The next time you visit a museum or some similar new (or even familiar) place, you could bring these mindfulness principles into practice. When you notice your mind reverting to recognition of the things you see and the stories associated with those things, pick your attention up and place it on something that you have never noticed before. Perhaps this would mean spending a few extra moments looking at a painting to notice something beyond the surface impression. Perhaps this means noticing the spaces around the art objects instead of the art itself. The invitation is to set aside preconceptions and open to what is present.

A few mindful breaths as you move from one room to another might help to ground you in the present. Since you are already walking, being aware of how your body feels as it walks through the space can likewise ground you in the now. While you look at the objects at hand and the spaces between, try to stay connected to your breath and body sensations as you are having the experience of seeing and listening. You just might be surprised by what you discover.

Culture

Since 1972 the Bhutanese have calculated GNH—Gross National Happiness. They are the only country to do so. Their culture is founded on Buddhist values and GNH comprises economic, environmental, physical, mental, workplace, social, and political *wellness*. They believe commerce should serve happiness. Here in the West, gross national product is the coin of the land. The Declaration of Independence guarantees "the pursuit of happiness," but in practice we seem to think that we've been guaranteed that happiness.

We are a dynamic mix of biology and culture. Our genetic makeup influences temperament and temperament influences how people, including our parents, respond to us. We live within multiple cultures—the larger cultures of West and East, developed versus developing nations, and regional and local cultures, including family cultures. The combination of cultures, biology, and experience provide us with predispositions from which we experience the world. While we can't undo our biology, we can examine the way that culture influences us and perhaps change that influence if we find it is not beneficial.

It may be difficult for us to find our own voice amid the tumult of cultural forces like advertising. It can be hard to distinguish what we really want from what we are supposed to want. Mindfulness can help us to make this distinction by helping us to know ourselves better. When we practice mindfulness our mind becomes an inner laboratory of experimentation. We study our experience and from this self-knowledge we have a better sense of what makes us tick—what our preferences are and how we want to be in the world. For example, if we are watching television and an advertisement comes on for a restaurant and we notice a quickening of our pulse and a desire arising for that pizza or whatever it is, we can pause and ask ourselves, "Am I really hungry now? Do I really want this?" Often, the answer will be no. The desire has been provoked by exposure to the enticing image. Self-knowledge trumps reaction.

Culture provides prepackaged meaning—narrative arcs for our lives—that we can adopt. For instance, the "American dream" suggests a prescription for living: Go to school, find a spouse, have children, work hard, move to the suburbs, buy lots of stuff, and go on vacations. Then we experience our kids growing up and doing the same. Retirement beckons—the "Golden Years." Of course, there is nothing wrong with pursuing the American dream. Our task, if we wish to bring mindfulness into our lives, is to live this dream with as much wakefulness as possible.

Mindfulness practice can connect us to new internal and external cultures. These cultures will be based on the values of awareness, generosity, and nonharmfulness. We may find some of this connection within ourselves. When we practice meditation, we might experience a loosening of the boundaries that define us. We can notice that the feelings of the breath are not limited to the breathing apparatus (nose, mouth, chest, lungs). The breath spreads throughout the body. We can notice, too, that we are not just this body—that we extend and exist in groups and even in connection to the planet. This is not an intellectual exercise or some New Age ideal of evolved consciousness. It is something that we can *actually* notice as we sit and meditate. We can perceive that we are in constant exchange with our environment and that we are part of larger communities extending beyond the skin that bounds our bodies. This sense of connectedness provides a context in which to view our consumerist culture. Do we really want all that stuff? Do we really *need* all that stuff?

We may find external cultural connection in a *Sangha*—a community of like-minded meditation practitioners who support each other by gathering to practice together. This culture may provide some respite from relentless want.

Curiosity

Dorothy Parker famously said, "The cure for boredom is curiosity. There is no cure for curiosity." Similarly, Marcel Proust wrote that "The real voyage of discovery consists not in seeing new landscapes, but in having new eyes." Both of these quotes capture what Zen teacher Shunryu Suzuki referred to as "the beginner's mind." Suzuki says, "In the beginner's mind there are many possibilities, in the expert's mind there are few." In other words, the beginner's mind is a form of engaged curiosity. It is an open frame of mind that has set aside preconceptions, agendas, and rules and that allows us to have a more direct experience of the moment. Despite claims that it killed the cat, a mindful curiosity can make our lives more vivid, exciting, and fascinating every time we look around or within ourselves.

Curiosity embraces a child-like quality when perceiving the world. If we can remove our habit of only perceiving things in reference to our own narratives, and of rendering uninteresting everything that is not central to what we think our story is, then we will be better able to see the ever-replenishing newness of the world. Every single thing encountered can then again become an opportunity for learning. Adults, in particular, can benefit from embracing a child-like, beginner's mind, which experiences more readily the uniqueness of unfolding events.

Montreal artist Sylvie Lupien takes close-up photographs of common objects worthy of Proust's "new set of eyes." Her work reveals the brilliant colors, forms, and textures that we typically fail to see in the most common, everyday objects. Many of her photographs are of ordinary objects in various states of decay. The freshness with which her eye sees what we typically consider to be the characterless backdrop of our world—the texture of peeling paint on plaster, graffiti against the rough surface of a brick wall, or the texture of aging upholstered fabric—reveals the beginner's mind. If we learn to look at our world with curiosity, we will begin to see new colors, forms, and textures in even the most mundane places that we have walked past a thousand times before.

We can use this same sort of curiosity in our own practice of mindfulness. We can become like anthropologists, observing our own experiences with detached curiosity. It is as if we are doing field study on ourselves. Our job is to observe and take notes. Good anthropologists don't analyze data until it's all collected. They don't jump to premature conclusions but are fascinated by nonjudgmentally observing human behavior. We can even take such a position with regard to things that are not going the way we want them to. If we can bring this same curiosity to our own experiences—especially to situations that are not going well—then we will be powerfully applying mindfulness in our lives.

We can begin to use curiosity as a tool for mindfulness with something small, like an itch.

- Let's say you are sitting in meditation and an itch arises.
- Your reflexive tendency is to scratch that itch, seeking immediate relief from the uncomfortable sensation.
- Curiosity would, instead, explore the itch—locate it; figure out what it is doing. "Oh, it's oscillating, how interesting."
- While you watch the itch do its thing, your irritation gradually dissolves and, at some point, so does the itch.

We can even bring curiosity to bear on something more adverse, like pain. Pain is a phenomenon happening now in the body. It may contain important information on tissue damage or illness, and in these cases we definitely want to be curious about it with an eye toward taking remedial action. But let's consider pain that falls into the category of chronic aches or the regular discomfort that arises when you sit in meditation. It can be handled in a similar way. Like the itch, it has a location and an oscillation. If you can set aside the story of how "terrible" it is, you will be able to open to the experience of it with a curious beginner's mind. Instead of the discomfort being a source of anguish, it can become a point of interest. Instead of trying to fix the discomfort or pain, you can relax into it and investigate its properties. Instead of fighting against it, you can accept that it is here and know that it will eventually dissolve. That's wisdom in action.

Death

Americans have a funny relationship with death. Mostly we deny it. While we know, at an intellectual level at least, that we are going to die, we don't know exactly when we will draw our final breath. The uncertainty surrounding the precise moment of our death is a stark reminder that our lives won't last forever. For some this is an unnerving and frightening thought, but for me it is good news. It wouldn't really be fun to live forever. We'd run out of things to say to each other!

The tentativeness of life makes it precious. All of our breaths come in pairs except for the first and the last. Each breath we take is one breath closer to our eventual last. This moment could be our last. Knowing this, we can be more deliberate in how we spend our moments. Life is a gift when we are awake to the eventuality of dying.

Unfortunately, despite our existential knowledge, we spend a lot of time in unwholesome states of being, like worry, regret, and complaint about what is happening now. If our time is short and uncertain, we might want to take advantage of every moment, appreciating what this moment has to offer. After all, this moment is the only place where we can actually live. We can remember the past and imagine the future but remembering and imagining are not *living*. Living is experiencing our senses and the creative capacities of our mind right now.

To bring death awareness into practice, we needn't look any farther than our own breathing. Our breath is a metaphor for the cycle of life. Each cycle of the breath is a mini lifecycle—coming into being and then dissolving into nothingness. It's a briefer version of the bigger picture. The arc of our lives reflects a similar process of becoming, abiding for a bit, and then dissolving. If we can be mindful of death as a part of the natural cycle of our life, we can relieve some of the fear it brings. The practice of mindfulness brings us intimately into the present moment of our lives. By remaining in touch with its fleeting moment-to-moment nature, we develop familiarity and a sense of peace with the transiency of life. In the end, when the final cycle comes, we will be better equipped to face it. Mindful living prepares us for mindful dying.

Death, which we usually imagine as happening in some other moment far in the future, will eventually arise as the present moment. The skill of mindfully facing the present moment, of releasing regret with regard to the past and fear with regard to the future, will provide us a sense of ease when death inevitably comes. We also gain the added benefit of not wasting the intervening moments of our lives between now and our departure focused solely on chasing from one desire to the next, but instead mindfully attending to what we have—friends, family, loved ones. Living without being caught up in the trap of desire, we will be ready to let go in any moment. It's all a matter of attitude, attention, and acumen—all skills of being awake.

Delusion

Buddha used fire as a metaphor for the emotional impulses that drive us to suffer. All of the myriad emotional states that disturb our peace of mind and burn up our happiness, he said, can be boiled down to three basic types: delusion, greed, and hatred. Greed and hatred in turn are said to erupt out of delusion. "Delusion" refers to a fundamental misperception of the world we live in, such that we mistakenly believe that it can grant us happiness, is reliably stable, and that the world and our experience of it are substantially real. The Buddha's contention was that if we look carefully, this world is actually unsatisfying, unreliable because it is constantly changing, and that there is no substantial bedrock of "self" to be found beneath its fleeting surfaces.

Delusion is called by many names—ignorance, confusion, bewilderment. I could write an entire book—a complete series of books—with anecdotes of "delusion." Every time I get angry, jealous, and feel self-pity, delusion can't be far away. Every time I feel morose, petty, and left out, ignorance is in the neighborhood. Every time I do things that bring harm upon others, the environment, and myself delusion is casting its shadow.

Greed and hatred can only happen to a self—a "me" that can want and not want. Confusion is dispelled when we understand that so long as craving and aversion are active, dissatisfaction, anguish, and suffering will permeate our every experience, waiting to flare up at the slightest upset. Ignorance is dispersed when we realize that everything is changing and there really is no "self" outside of the fleeting combination of ever moving factors that make up our momentary experiences.

Delusion can operate on the level of a single moment or a whole life, within an individual, a culture, or a world. Individual moments under the influence of delusion aggregate, snowball, and coalesce to make up an entire life. A life influenced by delusion can be lived alongside the lives of others influenced by delusion, and these lives in common form cultures influenced by delusion. Deluded cultures can make up the entire world. In this way, our world functions like the individual self on a much larger scale—it is a moving target of impulses, perceptions, and actions. It is only through counteracting delusion that we will make ourselves and our world a better place.

The Buddha understood that privilege and wealth did not bring him lasting happiness. Part of the problem is that we are naturally creatures of "hedonic adaptation." In other words, when we seek out and find pleasurable things, we initially experience a burst of satisfaction and happiness, but over time we grow accustomed to them and our happiness fades. If we win the lottery we get a boost in happiness and then return to our baseline everyday levels of happiness. If we lose our job, we get depressed and then, likewise, over time we'll return to our baseline levels of happiness. The natural durability of our baseline sense of happiness may help to explain why the pursuit of material objects and pleasurable experiences does not lead to enduring happiness. However, our baseline level of happiness is not absolutely fixed.

The practice of mindfulness, which helps us to be intimately aware of the fleeting nature of ourselves, our desires, and the objects of our desires, helps to dispel the delusion that leads to unhappiness. Just imagine, if everyone on the planet became mindful, most of the world's problems would likely dissipate. If everyone sought awakening and moved through the world, leading with goodness, the world would be a much better place. We can make our own contribution to the betterment of the world by dispelling a bit of our own delusion with mindfulness. Bringing mindfulness to bear in our own lives will not only help us to feel basically happier, by counteracting a modicum of the delusion in our world, it can lead to the happiness of others as well.

Dharma

When traveling in the Buddha's time, yogis would hail each other with, "Who's dharma do you follow?" Dharma meant a set of teachings from a particular teacher. The Buddha's dharma is set out in the voluminous Buddhist Canons, preserved in Pali, Sanskrit, Chinese, and Tibetan languages. The Buddhist Canons represent the written legacy of the discourses, sermons, and teachings that the Buddha delivered over his forty-five year teaching career. Dharma has another, deeper meaning. It refers to the way things are—the natural law of things. The laws of physics are dharma and the law of karma is dharma. The dharma of Buddha's teachings is meant to help us understand the dharma of reality.

If we were to summarize the Buddha's dharma in one phrase, it might be "Be good." The take-home message from Buddha's vast and profound set of interrelated teachings is that we should be good, be kind to others and ourselves, and move in the world with the goal of minimizing harm. This is the most direct teaching that the Buddha gave his followers. Of course, in order to be good, we must be able to pay attention to what is happening in the way that mindfulness provides. Although this dharma springs from the Buddha's understanding of the fundamental nature of reality, we need not penetrate that heady topic in order to practice goodness. In this sense, although the Buddha's dharma is quite profound, it is also quite simple.

There are three interrelated disciplines that form the foundation on which we may put the Buddha's dharma into practice: ethics (or living well), concentration (or meditation), and wisdom (or understanding things as they are). By wisdom is meant an understanding of the three flaws of existence—(1) that every experience is tinged with dissatisfaction, anguish, or suffering, (2) that everything is constantly changing and impermanent, and (3) that there is no real self, no real "I" standing outside of the flow of experience. The discipline of meditation is practiced to help us have a direct experience of these three facts. By meditating we come to more easily perceive the dissatisfaction, to notice the impermanence, and to see through the illusory "I" that drives us to suffer. The discipline of ethical living helps the mind to naturally settle and come to clarity. By refraining from chasing after desires, responding angrily when things don't go our way, and allowing ignorance to direct our behavior, much of what disturbs our minds ceases, and clarity is easily found. In this way, the three disciplines allow us to practice dharma—to be good, to act with greater kindness, and to avoid bringing harm into the world.

Our own practice of mindfulness can be a powerful means of cultivating this simple dharma of "being good." You can try this now by reflecting on the various experiences that a session of mindfulness brings. For example:

- When you bring your attention to your breathing, within a few moments you'll typically find that the mind has become involved in a story about the future, ruminating on the past, or opinionating about the present. When you are engaged with the stories about the future, the past, or the present you are likely to feel tension, anxiety, or restlessness. You worry about or anticipate what will happen, regret or relish what has happened, or are satisfied or dissatisfied with what is happening—in short, every experience is tinged with some kind of tension.

- As you settle into mindfully watching your attention as it moves from breathing to distraction and back again, you witness the fleeting impermanence of experience. And when attention is successfully sustained upon the breath you will notice the ever-changing qualities of something as seemingly stable as breathing—no two breaths are the same. In short, by mindfully paying attention we see that everything is constantly changing and impermanent.

- As the mind acclimates to a deeper and deeper sense that everything that we experience is ephemeral and transitory, you begin to notice that the "I" that lives at the heart of the stories that drive the roller coaster of anticipation, fulfillment, and regret is less substantial than it seems. The emptiness of the self—in other words, that there is no real "I" standing apart from transitory experience—even if only briefly glimpsed when attending mindfully to the process of breathing, is a profound fact that can change the way we are in the world.

By cultivating mindfulness we begin to notice that dissatisfaction actually comes from wishing things were other than they are in this moment. We exacerbate this desire by trying to hold on to the things we like and to push away the things we don't like, in spite of the fact that we know deep down that things cannot last. All this pushing and pulling gives rise to a sense of an "I" that seems to be standing outside the flow of experience as a truly existing, permanent recipient of pleasure or pain. When we have an unrealistic appreciation of ourselves in this way, we are liable to favor ourselves over others and to work for our benefit over the benefit of others.

The cultivation of mindfulness helps us to reduce this sense of self-importance, and to be more aware of our interconnectedness with others. We will be able to let go of aggravations and upsets, and to remember that the experiences that we don't enjoy are as impermanent as those we do. Being able to let go of expectations, constant judgments, and regrets will help to relieve a bit of our own suffering. Being able to think outside of the narrow perspective of "me, me, me," we will be able to think more of others, and thereby to live ethically. In this way, mindfulness can be our key to practicing the Buddha's simple dharma of "being good."

Distraction

As I drove through the campus of the University of Vermont the other day, I noticed how distracted students were with their handheld technology. A couple of students barely looked up from text messaging before stepping off the curb into the street, and it seemed as if every other student had a cell phone against her ear. Everyone was plugged in. Then I saw a squirrel crossing the road with an acorn in its mouth. Perhaps mobile devices have become our acorns: ubiquitous, culturally iconic, and indispensable.

We wile away our days with smartphones, emails, texts, status updates, and sometimes even old-fashioned phone calls. Many of us see these technologies as blessings, because they allow us to multitask and presumably get more done in the day. But they can also become a curse if we allow ourselves to become mindlessly obsessed with being connected. Such obsession even has a name—*infomania*. Infomaniacs constantly, uncontrollably check their devices, spend hours on Facebook and Twitter, and grow anxious—even frantic—if unplugged. They surreptitiously text during meetings, while driving, or under the family dinner table. They may even experience symptoms of withdrawal if cut off from the information stream.

I would like to suggest, as research does and contrary to popular opinion, that multitasking does not make us more efficient. In fact, having our attention constantly fragmented and interrupted each time an email, text, or tweet arrives makes us very inefficient. Each incoming notification distracts us from something else we were doing. Shifting our attention back and forth requires time, at the very least, and also disrupts our concentration on the task we had been engaged in. Old hard drives, when fragmented, would run inefficiently. It might be the same for our minds: when our attention is fragmented, we work much less efficiently.

We might think of mindfulness as a traditional means of defragging our attention. It works by collecting our attention into one task at a time—like simply observing the movement of the breath as we breathe. Of course, our attention won't stay there automatically, so we must bring it back when it strays. After all, attentions have been wandering for as long as we've had them, and there were plenty of distractions even in the Buddha's day. It may seem, with all the advances in technology and connectivity, that we live in the Age of Distraction, but the nature of the mind and attention is the same as ever despite the technological revolution. If we keep gently returning our attention to the breath each time it moves away, our ability to resist distraction and concentrate on the task at hand will grow stronger and stronger.

Occasionally unplugging from devices may help us to more easily overcome distraction. It may seem like a heretical suggestion, particularly if we are used to being plugged in twenty-four-seven, but it isn't the end of the world. I misplaced my cell phone for a couple of days once a few years ago and it turned out to be quite a liberating experience. More recently, one day I forgot to bring my iPhone with me to work. After the initial pangs of anxiety, I enjoyed the spaciousness and freedom that came with being inaccessible.

It would be hard for me to permanently give up my technology, but we don't need to do that in order to overcome distraction. To better manage distraction, we need to first see how pervasive its effects on us are. The quantity of interactions we gain from being constantly connected may cost us when it comes to the quality of those exchanges. It is hard to be fully present with friends, family members, and associates or to fully enjoy experiences as we have them when a large part of our mind is elsewhere. Once we recognize what constant distraction costs us, we can learn how to minimize its effects by setting aside a block of time each day when we put away our smartphones and cultivate our ability to attend to our present experience instead. This is meditation. If distraction has become a particular problem, we may want to go away on a meditation retreat where we relinquish all of our technologies (including reading and writing) for an extended period of time to focus intensely on attending to ourselves. Then we'd really be unplugged!

I've heard that there are computer programs that restrict one from accessing the internet for designated periods of time. A regular practice of mindfulness meditation can accomplish the same thing. We could also choose to skillfully use our plugged-in-ness to foster mindfulness. Try this: each time your technology "talks" to you—the phone rings, a text message chimes, an email arrives in your inbox—take a mindful breath before attending to it. We can be both plugged in *and* mindful.

Dukkha

Anguish is a pervasive feature of human life. Siddhartha Gautama, the Buddha before he became the Buddha, observed this millennia ago— and it continues today, despite all the advancements of the twenty-first century. For the young Siddhartha, it wasn't that life was just difficult— riddled with disease, aging, and death—something more pernicious infected every moment of existence, even those that were pleasurable.

Something was off. He wanted to push away the unpleasant and hold on to the pleasant, but he couldn't succeed at this because everything was always changing. He set out to find a way to overcome his anguish and found it—in no small part, by developing mindfulness.

The Buddha referred to this experience as *dukkha* and it encompasses anguish as well as a range of other feelings: stress, misery, dissatisfaction, and suffering. You may see dukkha translated as any of these terms but it is really a metaphor. Dukkha means "bad" or "broken wheel." It is a wheel that is off its axle or bent and out of true. When he gave his first teachings, the Buddha likened the human condition to an ox cart with that ill-fitting and wobbly wheel. Though one may occasionally take pleasure in the diversion of the ride, the effects of that one bad wheel mar the overall experience. The wheel causes the cart to sway, lurch, and drag along the road. A similar "offness" permeates every moment of our experience, and there is no escaping it without a fundamental change in attitude.

Something is off. We can't quite put our finger on it, especially those of us in affluent societies. Our bellies are full, we have great material wealth and pleasure, yet happiness remains elusive. We find ourselves surrounded with abundance—everything we could possibly desire at our fingertips—and yet we are still plagued by unhappiness. We must logically look somewhere other than the outside world for the source of our anguish. We can't pin this "offness" on our circumstances. The culprit, rather, seems to be in our minds—the constant conversation, chatter, and complaints that populate our inner mental space, working to continually judge and color each experience that passes before us.

Life can be difficult, of course. Sickness, old age, and death are as salient now as they were in ancient India. But how we relate to disappointment, loss, and setbacks in our life determines to a large extent whether we feel dukkha as a result of them. We can choose to relate to our experiences through the elaborative drama of "story" or through the naked simplicity of perception. "Why is this happening to me?" "What did I do to deserve this?" "Poor me." Such is the work of our inner storyteller: sensationalist self-talk that complicates the situations of our lives. Instead of experiencing events just as they are, we embellish them with our personal hopes and fears, adding a layer of anguish. Situations become problems. Problems become crises.

So instead of choosing to weave ourselves into a story, we can approach our problems through simple perception. If we don't choose a story, we won't feel anguish. Pain may be present but not the anguished suffering that comes from relating to events in our lives in an overly personal manner. Anguish yields to equanimity. When dukkha is quieted, nirvana is present.

Not too long ago, the *quadratus lumborum* muscle in my lower back began to spasm while I was at work. It felt as if a large-gauge wire had been inserted into my side, pumping out hot electricity. The pain was so intense I became nauseous and my body shook. I had a long day ahead and decided to soldier on because a spasm, such as this, often resolves itself. But this one did not. It grew more intense throughout the day. I soon found that there was not room enough to do my work listening to people *and* to engage in fear, resistance, and complaint. The pain riveted me to the present moment, even though it was not a pleasant one.

Those particular sensations could have given rise to anguish at any moment, and in many moments that day they did. But once I recognized those moments of anguish, I touched them with mindfulness and the anguish released. I would go from being unhappy to just being in that particular embodied state. I would go from feeling trapped to being back in the moment. I knew that the agony was impermanent; eventually it would relent. I would be fine. My practice of mindfulness gave me the strength to endure hours of penetrating pain with some degree of equanimity. Later that evening the pain finally relented. The same principles of mindful attention can be applied to emotional pain as well as to physical pain. In this way, mindfulness can help transform the anguish of dukkha into acceptance.

Eating

When I was in India, living and studying at an ashram (a spiritual practice center), I loved the indigenous cuisine. We'd eat lunch sitting on the floor in rows, our meals skillfully ladled from gleaming stainless steel pots onto a banana leaf. One day there was a festival, accompanied by a special self-serve meal. I saw what looked like mashed potatoes and excitedly took a heaping portion, since I hadn't seen them since I'd been in India. Much to my surprise and chagrin they were not mashed potatoes but an intense, rich, cardamom-laced dessert that would have been perfect in a small serving but overwhelming in the gluttonous way it was sitting on my plate. Not wanting to waste the food I had hastily taken, I ate it all. I had a bellyache for a long time after.

It makes sense to pay attention to what we are eating, in particular to know precisely what it is that we are eating, how much of it we are consuming, and how the food might affect us. Too often, however, mindfulness and eating are not companions. We talk while we eat. We drive while we eat. We watch television, surf the web, tweet, and work while we eat. We eat lunch at our desks, paying no attention whatsoever to the meal or to the process of eating it. Truthfully, I am even munching on my morning cereal as I write this.

Since we eat every day, we can easily use this regular activity as an opportunity to practice a bit of mindfulness. In fact, mindful eating was the very first mindfulness exercise taught at the Stress Reduction

Clinic in 1979 by Jon Kabat-Zinn. It is a very simple practice that involves paying attention to the experience of eating: its sights, sounds, textures, smells, and flavors. Kabat-Zinn famously used a raisin as the piece of food with which to introduce the practice.

- Place the raisin in the palm of your hand and look at it as if you've never seen it before. It's true, too. You've never seen this particular raisin before.
- Appreciate its physical properties—its color and shape, and the way it reflects the light.
- Next, take it in your fingers and appreciate the feel of its texture.
- If you roll it next to your ear you might hear a sound—perhaps a small crinkle.
- Now, place it under your nose and appreciate the aroma.
- You are almost ready to put it in your mouth. First, place it on the tip of your tongue. Resist the urge to bite into it. Explore the texture again, now with your tongue. Notice everything that is happening in your mouth, especially the salivation.
- Next take a bite, appreciate the flavors, and chew slowly. Take your time in doing this.
- If your attention is distracted by thoughts about the future, the past, or by internal commentary about the present experience, gently bring it back to the bare experience of the raisin.

Giving our full attention to the experience of eating causes us to slow down while we eat. Mindful eating is an effective means of bringing a bit of order to our disordered eating habits, especially to impulsive, unconscious, binge eating. This makes sense, as it's hard to overeat when we are eating with slow, attentive deliberation. We can apply the simple practice of mindful eating, here applied to a raisin, to our regular meals as well.

Begin by taking a few moments to appreciate the food that you have before you begin eating. It took countless events to make this food available to you: rain, bacteria, farmers, truckers, and the supermarket clerk all contributed to its existence on your plate. Take a moment to appreciate the fact that this food will sustain your body and give you the chance to live mindfully. Reflect on the fact that our ancestors had to work hard to secure food, hunting and gathering under uncertain conditions. Having a full belly was never a given for them; getting enough to eat was often a major accomplishment. Cultivating this awareness can help us not to take eating for granted. If we take our food for granted, we may end up eating with little or no awareness of how lucky we are to have plenty and how meaningful each bite can be.

Then give your full attention to the experience of eating each bite of your meal, following the same steps used with the raisin. Let your eyes take in the appearance of each bite, your nose take in its aroma, and your tongue take in its taste and texture. Listen to the sounds that it makes as you chew. Take a bite of food and then place your spoon or fork down on the table. Don't pick it up again until you have finished chewing and swallowing what is in your mouth. If your mind drifts from the immediate process of eating, gently return it.

Eating in this way slows things down. Deliberately attending to eating allows us to better appreciate the food that we have, and allows the process of eating to function as it should: what we eat reaches our stomachs and our stomachs signal our brains that they have been sufficiently fed before we have mindlessly overeaten. We also gain the added benefit of enjoying our food more as we savor it with full attention.

Effort

Contrary to what we might think, the brain is not quiet during meditation; it is highly activated, albeit in a different way than it commonly is. Meditation requires great effort—sitting still, concentrating, and returning attention each time it moves away. This effort requires energy before it can give energy back. It takes discipline, commitment, and persistence to maintain a daily practice.

If we try too hard, our effort can actually get in the way of what we are trying to accomplish. Striving after a goal can become an obstacle in itself. Mindfulness practice requires that we not strain for results; that we not reach for particular experiences. Mindful effort is more about *allowing* something to happen than it is about toiling to make it so. Allowing may initially feel counterintuitive, especially if we are accustomed to doing everything in an achievement-oriented way.

In traditional lists of practices used on the Buddhist path, we find one named "Right Effort." Effort that is "right" sets us in a beneficial direction, gives us a nudge forward, and then allows us to proceed with the work at hand with no further agenda. Our work is accomplished by setting well our intention and is better achieved when evaluation, judgment, and commentary are left aside as it unfolds.

What does it mean to engage in meditation with energy and without having some result as our goal? How do we make effort without striving? When I sit, I know that it feels very different *how* I sit. When I slump a bit, my energy feels dull. When I keep my hips forward and my shoulders up, I feel nobler. I also feel more open, even vulnerable. This puts me in a better place for practice since I am not hunkered down in a self-protective mode. It takes patience to retrieve my restless mind over and over again. It takes an intellectual effort to hold a wisdom frame of mind that tries not to identify with what is happening as "my meditation experience" but rather the passing experience of each moment. It takes persistence to stay on the cushion when my body gets tired, restless, and sore. Often, too, it requires effort to get myself on the cushion in the first place. Here, I may have to push through some resistance that doesn't feel like practicing.

But trying too hard can take us out of the moment. Pushing so hard that our practice becomes a struggle adds an element of expectation, which is a form of fantasizing about a particular future outcome.

Grinding does not allow things to be as they are. This is the quandary of effort: we need to try without trying too hard. We must apply just the right amount of direction and focus to sustain our practice, but not to disrupt it.

We may need to encourage ourselves gently in the direction of practice. Challenges arise. Daily life is complicated and busy; it may seem like we have no time to practice. But the effort required to be mindful in any given moment is small. After we bring our attention to what is happening now, the onrush of life works to pull us back into our story. Effort is the aggregate of many small moves, many small corrections in the direction of attending to the here and now. It is not about forcing our minds to stand still like statues. It's about simply bringing attention back again and again. Good effort is the art of the gentle return to now.

Emotional Intelligence

Up until the fifth grade, I got into a lot of trouble in school. I always got poor marks for behavior. Most of my teachers did not know how to handle my exuberance, defiance, and boredom. When I acted out, my first grade teacher, Mrs. Percy, would send me to the kindergarten class. My "punishment" was to read to them. In the fourth grade Mrs. Barrcelli, a long-term substitute, sent me to the principal's office on a regular basis. It wasn't until the fifth grade that my first male teacher, Mr. Andreosky, began to set limits on my misbehavior and help me get a handle on my emotions. One day I was goofing off with a buddy of mine, Kenny. Mr. A caught us and said, "Kozak, you and Messink are going to be the outstanding players at this week's kickball game. You'll be *out standing* by the fence when everyone else is playing!" This was an early lesson that my actions had consequences and that I could modify my behavior to get preferred outcomes. I never missed another kickball game.

It is unfortunate that we were never explicitly taught how to identify, value, and use our emotions for our betterment. Emotional intelligence (EI) has only recently become a cultural buzzword. EI is used to refer to everything from self-esteem and enthusiasm to calmness and ease. But it has a more specific meaning that dovetails nicely with mindfulness. EI is our ability to be aware of our emotional life—to access and use the information from our feelings to guide our thinking and behavior. To be emotionally intelligent, we must first be able to recognize when we are having feelings, identify what they are, and manage them in a way consistent with our goals, values, and aspirations. We become emotionally intelligent when we become aware of our affective life and use that awareness for the benefit of others and ourselves.

EI comprises four interrelated abilities: the skills of perceiving emotions accurately, using emotions to facilitate thoughtful reflection, understanding what our emotions mean, and managing them when they occur. The more in touch with our feelings we become, the more rational we can be. With the development of skills, we can recruit our feelings to attain specific goals. Neuroscientist Antonio Damasio tells us that people who have lost their ability to process emotions due to brain damage cannot reason in certain domains. Being rational in the world requires an intact feeling system. Rationality without feelings can't exist.

Excessive desire, hatred, and confusion are at odds with an emotionally intelligent life. Desire can hijack our better interests in the service of pursuing selfish goals. We may become so blinded by craving that we don't see things clearly. We can become obsessive, consumed with chasing ends that we presume will satisfy our longing. We may do things that are destructive, irrational, and futile. When the three fires of desire, hatred, and delusion engulf us, we lose control of ourselves and may experience emotional outbursts, much like children. Such outbursts can be "expensive" because they exhaust our energy and can lead to collateral social costs, such as inconveniencing, insulting, or even harming others.

Developing mindfulness can help us to develop EI because, as a byproduct of paying attention to our minds from moment to moment, we become intimate with our emotional life. We learn to manage our emotions by being mindful of their arising energy and, with that awareness, we are less likely to be blindsided and more likely to make good choices.

Energy

I remember watching *The Newlywed Game* as a child. I couldn't have been more than ten or twelve. One spouse was asked the question (and I paraphrase), "If you were able to have sufficient energy would you give up sleeping?" Even then, I was affirmative on that question. I wanted to be awake around the clock—there was so much that I wanted to do. Forty or so years later, I still fantasize about that possibility. Imagine all that I could get done! But while I often wish that I had more time, what I really want is the energy to better use the time I have.

Many things can affect energy—sleep or lack of sleep, of course, is one of the primary factors. Other factors, including our interactions with others, what we put into our bodies, and what goes on in our internal headspace, also affect our energy levels. Our minds can have a great impact on how much energy we have. In fact, neuroscientist Dan Siegel defines the mind as a "relational and embodied process that regulates the flow of energy and information." Everything we experience is an energy exchange.

Mindfulness will help us to see if this process is flowing in a beneficial way—leading to increased energy. Notice, for example, how you feel after interactions with others. In some cases, you may feel energized, and in others you may feel drained. Some people leave you feeling open and engaged, and others leave you feeling closed off, as if in retreat. The quality of the attention we bring to such interactions will affect the dynamics of the energy exchange that takes place. When we are fully present—to ourselves and to those we interact with—we will be better able to manage the energetic cost of our interactions, even with a difficult person.

In some situations, we have a choice about whom we interact with; we can engage those people who energize us and avoid those who don't. However, many times we don't have the convenience of choice. We have to talk to our bosses, coworkers, and family members. These interactions really challenge us to be mindful—to stay grounded in the body and to pay attention to how our attitude shapes the encounter. If we can approach such encounters with an attitude of interest, as an objective observer, we can bring a measure of equanimity to it. The same can be applied to what goes on in our internal headspaces. We have the ability to intervene in our thoughts, to redirect attention away from storytelling to the present moment. It is quite challenging to bring mindfulness into real time interactions, but formal practice on the cushion provides the training that will support such a practice.

Most of what we do during the day requires a healthy amount of energy in order to succeed: work, relationships, play, creativity. Poor energy can lead to halfhearted engagement, and halfhearted engagement can lead to exhaustion. When we feel low on energy, our impulse might be to do something mindless rather than something mindful to restore our energy. Watching television does not require much energy from us, and this is perhaps why it is so appealing after a long day of work. It is doubtful, however, that watching television will give us energy. It may seem counterintuitive, but spending a few moments practicing mindfulness can actually help us recharge at the end of a long day.

Mindfulness practice can lead to increased energy as we relate to ourselves in the exquisitely attuned way that unfolds during practice. In a very direct sense, mindfulness practice is the ongoing investigation of energetic patterns as they manifest as sensations in the body. As we practice, we shift our attention from the concept of who we are to the actual experience of who we are—a living, dynamic, and changing being. Our practice is to attend to this flow of energy and information and to see it for what it is.

Concepts like "I" and "mine" grow out of the experiences grounded in our body. We weave stories about what is happening to us based on the pleasant and painful experiences rooted in the body. When the story takes a turn toward something we dislike, we are apt to experience all sorts of emotions. Anxiety, for instance, is embedded in a story about what might or might not happen, and it can be traced to its energy signature somewhere in the body. While it is unlikely that we will be able to eradicate anxiety altogether, we can work to extricate ourselves from the storytelling that exacerbates it by recognizing the difference between sensations in the body and the fictions we weave around them.

When you notice that your mind is engaged in an anxiety-related story that is draining you of energy, pay attention to the bodily sensations underneath the anxiety. Let go of the story and attend solely to the various sensations as they come and go, rise and fall, and evolve. Pay attention to that energy. Breathe into it and through it. When you are able to cease elaborating the story, the anxiety cannot persist. In this way mindfulness can be a great technique for managing energy-draining experiences like anxiety and helping us to be more efficient in terms of how we spend our mental and physical energy.

Engagement

I am washing the pots and pans after lunch at the Barre Center for Buddhist Studies, my brief volunteer yogi job. I love washing dishes. I work quietly, my wandering mind contained by attending to the task at hand. Time stops as I engage with the multisensory actions of cleaning the smooth metal surfaces. The water warms my hands, wrists, and forearms; I am working to be efficient yet not rushed. My mind becomes quiet—silent—just this pot and then the next. When the pots are all clean, I feel a sense of accomplishment. I've contributed to the greater good of our little community.

Silence, containment, and engagement make up the Holy Trinity of mindfulness. The practice of mindfulness automatically brings a measure of silence into our lives. Silence provides us the opportunity to taste stillness, to just be with the moment as it is. Resting in the moment helps us not to act on impulse. Our behavior becomes contained. Containment does not mean suppression, but rather that we are not pushed around by our thoughts and emotions. Rather than cutting us off from life, containment gives us the chance to engage it more fully without disruptions brought on by unruly thoughts and emotions. When we are engaged life becomes more vivid. Sights, sounds, smells, tastes, and bodily sensations seem more available. Even the most ordinary circumstances become engaging. Something as pedestrian as breathing can be fulfilling beyond words.

Without even realizing it, we may end up drifting through our lives half asleep, not really engaging it. Much of what we do during the day can be done on automatic pilot—walking, eating, driving, and so on. While our ability to do things unconsciously may help civilization to proceed apace, it disconnects us from being fully alive. When we do not engage fully with the day-to-day run of our lives, we end up simply going through the motions. The longer we live in this half-asleep way, the more exhausted we feel, despite the fact that we aren't really doing much. As the Benedictine monk Brother David Stendhal Rast said, as relayed by David Whyte in his audio series *Clear Mind, Wild Heart,* "The antidote to exhaustion is not necessarily rest; the antidote is wholeheartedness." If we are halfhearted, we are cut off from meaning, purpose, and energy. A halfhearted approach to life is exhausting. Wholehearted dedication means spending more time with what is happening while investing less energy in pursuing the stories and opinions that distract us from it.

Our days provide countless opportunities to engage. If we make the choice to engage with the world around us, we might find that joy, creativity, and energy naturally emerge.

Consider a fully engaged, mindful morning:

- When you wake up and stretch, make an effort to really feel the sensations of your body. Let your mind just inhabit your body, rather than running immediately to the day's to-do list.

- Do a brief scan of your body: note any tension, soreness, or warmth in your muscles and joints as you internally sweep your mind from the top of your head to the tips of your toes.
- Be mindful of how you move as you get up, swinging your legs over the side of the bed. What a miracle it is to be able to move in this way!
- Place your attention on a few cycles of breathing.
- Carry this mindfulness of the body into whatever you do next.

Mornings provide the best opportunities for engagement. The to-do list can wait. We can give our full attention to moving, eliminating, washing, dressing, and whatever else we do as we prepare for the rest of our day. Each time attention moves into the to-do list, we can come back to the sensations appreciable now—for example, the touch of the toothbrush in the mouth, the taste of the toothpaste, the swirling sensations of water as we rinse. The two minutes we are supposed to be brushing our teeth can be two minutes spent engaged with mindfulness—a great way to start the day.

Enlightenment

Enlightenment is not a destination; you don't arrive through a gate emblazoned with "nirvana," set up camp, and live there forever. We may imagine enlightenment as some grandiose, transcendental sphere beyond our world, in which case we may well be disappointed should we attain it. It's nothing special. Each time we are mindful we approximate enlightenment: just this moment as it is. It's not necessarily a peak experience with fireworks, bliss, and transcendence. It may come so unexpectedly that we might even overlook it. As Dinty Moore says in *The Mindful Writer*, "You can't plan for enlightenment. It doesn't arrive like frequent flyer rewards."

When Siddhartha Gautama emerged from his days and nights under the Bodhi tree, he did not say that he was enlightened. Rather, he said that he was "awake." And so he came to be called "Buddha," which means the Awakened One. The English words "enlightenment" and "awakening" have different implications. "Enlightenment" suggests something sudden, luminescent, and exotic. We like the idea that illumination comes quickly, and that once it happens, we're done, but such ideas are likely unrealistic. "Awakening," on the other hand, suggests something natural and commonplace that happens to us each morning. Buddha's choice to use awakening as a metaphor for his experience is quite apt. We live our lives as if we are asleep, lost in dreams of what might have been, what could be instead, and what should be later, rather than being awake to the bare, immediate reality of now.

The psychologist Richard Keefe had the following to say about enlightenment in his book *On the Sweet Spot: Stalking the Effortless Present*:

> Mystical experience is often depicted with images of heavenly light raining on a subject from above, or the twinkling of auras around his or her soul. In reality, it's much grittier than that. Mystical experience is characterized by a dramatic shift in attention to the richness of the present. The hands of the mystic are not always clean; they are covered with the earthiness of the moment, and the mystic feels his hands fully, whether they are dipped in mud or dabbed with blood.

Keefe's description is of an enlightenment that is more available and less idealized. In our day-to-day lives, we have our hands in the mud all the time: enlightenment is hidden right here in plain sight in the mundane experiences we habitually bury under elaborate stories. Perhaps enlightenment is no big deal and is right here beneath our nose waiting for our attention.

Enlightenment is experienced in those moments wherein we let go of the impulse to add opinions, commentaries, or agendas that seek to improve or alter our experience. Although we are talking about not doing something, it turns out that it is quite difficult, nearly impossible, to achieve due to longstanding mental habits. It's very hard to simply be with an experience without wanting to narrate it, compare it to other experiences, or in some way elaborate on it. We are always adding something, even if we think an experience is perfect as it is. Even when we manage to avoid gross elaboration, we are likely to add to our experience a subtle desire to freeze it, to hold on to it.

We all engage in a ceaseless lean and tug with what we experience. If we can manage to stop pushing and pulling, then we will find nirvana. A lifetime of conditioning and ages of human evolution make it quite difficult to simply discontinue such tendencies. We naturally add to our experiences, without even trying.

The practice of mindfulness is the practice of noticing additions, of being able to recognize the difference between experience itself and our elaboration of it. With mindfulness we learn to recognize embellishments and to redirect our attention back to the simple feeling of the breath in this very moment. When we can be with our breath, just as it is, naked and embodied, then we taste a bit of enlightenment. We will likely waver, from moment to moment, between storytelling and being fully present. Mindfulness presents us the opportunity, rather than grow aggravated at this fluctuation of attention, to simply turn our attention back to the breath again. As such, our practice becomes the practice of touching enlightenment again and again, if only for a moment at a time.

Equanimity

Mindfulness is often marketed with images of a drop of water rippling out over a smooth expanse. I've used such pictures myself in advertising the mindfulness programs that I teach. The image is useful as visual shorthand because it suggests the stereotype of equanimity—tranquil, peaceful, and serene. While equanimity can embody these characteristics, it is a simplification of the idea to say the least. A fuller picture of equanimity would convey that equanimity is more than simple serenity, it engages in the nitty-gritty challenges of moment-to-moment existence.

Equanimity requires that we learn to attend to what is happening without reacting to it excessively—without developing craving or aversion for experiences. By finding a balance in between extreme reactions, we can learn to notice what is happening within and around us without losing control of how we respond to it. Rather than seeing challenging experiences as threats to our well-being, we can learn to approach them with a bit of equanimity, noting challenges and responding to them in a way that doesn't compound the difficulty of the moment.

The meditation teacher Shinzen Young defines equanimity as the effort to "let go of negative judgments about what you are experiencing and replacing them with an attitude of loving acceptance and gentle matter-of-factness." In finding balance, we neither avoid the difficult nor identify too closely with it. From an equanimous point of view, we neither fixate on nor run away from what is happening. We don't get in the way of the inevitable rise and fall of each experience. Equanimity is not apathy or flatness; we could think of it instead as a balanced, judgment-free interest.

When considered from a position of equanimity, we can bring an attitude of balanced interest to our experiences—whether pleasant or unpleasant, easy or difficult, mundane or extraordinary. Rather than losing ourselves in reactions to events, we simply attend to the particulars of what is happening, its characteristics, and how it changes from moment to moment. It is hard to be distressed when we remain detached from what is happening. Distress bubbles up out of the stories we weave with "me" at the center. Equanimity mutes the drama of storytelling so that in place of anxiety we find perception.

Someone I work with had a bad fall just before Christmas. She deals with severe chronic pain, so a broken ankle would be an especially unwelcomed thing. Since she had been practicing mindfulness for some time, she was better prepared to deal with an unexpected situation. Practice helped her to move to equanimity. The experience became a breakthrough of insight rather than a disaster. As she was falling to the floor, time slowed, and she did not relate to the sensations through the lens of "me." She was interested in everything that was happening—the changing planes of vision as she moved toward the floor, the sheering of bone and tearing of flesh. While she had great pain, she did not have great suffering. Her insight emerged from a radical shifting of perception away from self that sustained her through recovery. It helped to stave off despair and kept her focus on the task at hand—healing.

Like good scientists, we can learn to observe any experience, even those that are terrible, without injecting them with our narratives. We can learn to observe with objectivity. We can learn to live through difficulties without making them worse. In charged interpersonal situations, if we can avoid anger or indignation, our calmness in the face of chaos might just be what allows productive communication to happen. The upsetting event is just something that is happening, after all. With a bit of equanimity we can choose how to respond to it, rather than it choosing for us.

Buddha spoke of life's hardships as two arrows. The first arrow is the losses and setbacks that we all experience in life. The second arrow, which often follows on the first, is our judgment and reaction to the first arrow, which tends only to further compound our suffering. Cultivating equanimity gives us the skill to face any situation, no matter how difficult, without adding further anguish. Equanimity is the balm that relieves the wound of the second arrow.

Experience

There is a low-lying rock wall outside my back door. It is old and worn and is falling apart. The settling stones have left gaps that local chipmunks have made their home. When I see the wall, I see something that I need to fix. But when my cat looks at the wall, he sees a bustling hive of potentially edible critters. We both look at the same wall, but we see it in very different ways. It's not just that he's a cat and I'm a human. Other humans, depending on what they bring with them, will see different things too—an interesting subject for a budding photographer, a seat for a tired worker, a place to play for a child.

Much of what we experience is not the "real world" that is out there waiting for us to find it. We participate in our perception of the world. The world that we experience is influenced by what we bring to it. We help to construct the world of our experience. This doesn't mean we are free to construct whatever we want willy-nilly: we won't be able to walk through walls, fly, or make a car into an elephant. What constructedness means is that we play a part in the perceived quality of our own experiences in the world. Clinging too greatly to our experience of the pleasantness or unpleasantness or worth or lack of worth of things and events in the world can lead to trouble, because such perceptions are not objective.

Recognizing the constructedness of experience is humbling. It helps me to understand that my immediate perceptions, emotions, and thoughts about things and events may not be accurate. I know that I too participate in the creation of my experience of things and that I don't have a privileged perspective. I'm trying to make sense of experience, just like everyone else. Every moment of life is an experience, whether it comes sitting on a meditation cushion or snowboarding down a snow-covered mountain, and the experiencer almost always colors the experience.

Experience starts with sensation. Our sensory organs process energies from the world around us—light striking the retina or sound waves vibrating our eardrums. As humans we can only see light within a certain range of the electromagnetic spectrum. We cannot see infrared as bats can, nor can we hear the high-pitched sounds that dogs can hear. These limitations to perception tell us there is more to the world beyond the range of our senses. The world is not just the way it appears to us. And after the limited portion of what is actually out there is transduced by our senses, it all must be processed by neural networks in our brains that have been habituated over our lifetime. This means that prior experience, learning, and expectations will color what is actually perceived. The brain interprets what the eyes see. Experience is not an absolute truth.

Perception is further influenced by attention. Even if some external stimuli impinges upon our sensory organs, we may not even perceive them if our attention is distracted. Our attention is very limited. In each second our sensory organs are processing millions of bits of information, but we are only conscious of few of them. We may even be less aware of what our senses receive from the environment if we are caught up in fantasizing about the future or ruminating about the past.

The practice of mindfulness helps us to perceive more truly, even though our experiences will still largely be filtered through language, learning, and mood. By rooting ourselves in the now, we are able to understand our experiences more clearly, to discern the difference between our perspective and what is real. When we cut through distractions, expectations, and habitual thought patterns we gain a richer experience that is closer to the truth. When our experience is more real it becomes more authentic, profound, and meaningful.

Fantasy

I am sitting in meditation. My stomach lets my brain know that I am hungry. I begin to think about the lunch waiting for me after the sitting—homemade local free-range savory fried chicken with fresh herbs from the garden. I begin to salivate. Without even realizing it, I have begun to lean forward, as if a racer ready to leap from the starting blocks. But I notice the diversion and refix my focus, investigating this sudden salivation and craving for food. What is its quality? Where does it arise in me bodily? How does it change over time? My exploration mutes the intensity of the distraction, and I gain a modicum of equanimity toward the craving. A few moments later the hunger pang resurges and I stray to fantasies of fried chicken again. "Man, it's going to be delicious!" So it goes for the forty-five minute practice—moving back and forth between fantasy and reality.

Years ago, a public service announcement used to appear nightly on local television stations: "It's ten p.m. Do you know where your children are?" When beginning a session of meditation, I mentally make a similar announcement to myself: "It's right now. Do I know where my mind is?" It sounds funny, but asking myself this question is a way to check my tendency to mentally wander into fantasy. Chances are that at any given moment we are not fully focused on what we are presently doing. Our attention leans toward the future, leaping ahead to the rest of the day, worrying about what's left on the daily to-do list. Or we drag along the past, mulling over what happened last night or what we should have done instead in this or that bygone situation. When we manage to reside in the present we are apt to get wrapped up in commentary about what's happening, wishing it last longer or hoping it will end soon. So, though it may sound funny, it is necessary to ask yourself at the beginning of a session of practice, "Do I know where my mind is?"

There is something you are doing now—in this case, reading. That is the activity of the moment. The information coming through your senses as you read this reflects your present reality. Everything else is fantasy. It is true that thoughts, images, and emotions can color our experience of the landscape of now. But our tendency is to perceive our thoughts and feelings about the present as part and parcel of the experience itself. We get caught up in stories that lead us farther and farther afield from the here and now. We mistake the process of relating to reality as the content of reality. In the end, our reality is obscured by fantasyland.

It is quite possible to live most of our lives in fantasy. We can navigate the world effectively doing so. We can maintain jobs, raise children, and do all the things that our harried lives demand, mostly on automatic pilot, our minds lost in stories about future, the past, or the present. Reality can be harsh. Fantasy can be lovely—an escape from the ugliness of the so-called "real-world." But in chasing after fantasies that are more interesting or exciting, we may be selling reality short. Even the difficult aspects of reality can turn out to be deeply compelling when attended to with interest.

Fantasy is inherent to who we are. The ability to imaginatively represent things that are not immediately present is one of the distinguishing features of the human mind. We have the capacity to imagine, and imagination can create symphonies, poetry, and technological advancement. It can also create worry, regret, and ceaseless desire. Fantasy can easily become a powerful addiction. In fact, it lies at the root of many others: we drink because we imagine it will make us more gregarious or fun; we take drugs because we imagine that we'll find enlightenment or ecstasy that way; we look at pornography imagining we will find more desirable or satisfying pleasure there. If we aren't attentive to our use of fantasy, we can lose touch with reality entirely.

Mindfulness meditation requires that we spend some time hanging out with reality—being with things as they actually are rather than trying to make them into something else. Mindfulness invites us to bring our attention fully to whatever is happening now, just as it is.

- Get into the habit of asking yourself, "What is happening now? What am I experiencing within and around myself? What are the qualities of the various colors, shapes, sounds, smells, and physical sensations that I encounter now? What are the qualities of my mental reactions or interactions with these stimuli? Can I be fully here to experience this?"
- When you are meditating, simply meditate.
- When you are walking, simply walk.
- When you are eating, simply eat.
- Whatever you do, do it with a full investment of attention.
- If your attention becomes dispersed in fantasy, simply note that it has happened, and gently return to the action at hand.

Don't beat yourself up when attention is dispersed by fantasy. It is quite natural to slip into imagination. This is our habitual mode of being, after all. Hanging out with reality, just as it is, may seem challenging at first because of this. This is why mindfulness is called a "practice." It takes practice to replace old habits with new ones. With practice, we embark on the process of becoming mindful of ourselves in the moment over and over again. Over time you may find that reality surpasses fantasy in every way.

Fascination

My cat finds subtle rustlings in the baseboards fascinating—perhaps a mouse to play with? Most other noises leave him nonplussed. As an animal, he doesn't have much choice about what captures his attention. As humans, however, we can choose our own objects of fascination. We can even choose to be fascinated by the most ordinary of things. The critical turn depends upon attention.

We are built to appreciate the novel aspects of experience. However, novelty seeking can become an end in itself. Without being aware of it, we may come to feel that our lives must perpetually include something new, something exciting. If this way of relating to life continues for prolonged periods, our short attention spans reduce the typical fifteen minutes of fame to fifteen seconds. We end up like mayflies, our attention constantly flitting from thing to thing, landing on nothing for more than a moment before quickly moving on.

As an alternative to the continual pursuit of superficial fascination, we can seek a more substantial and profound fascination right under our noses. All we need do is rest our attention on the simple rhythm of our breathing. The regular, cyclic rhythm of the breath as it moves in and out of our bodies can be downright fascinating if we just permit ourselves to attend to it. The miracle of life—perpetually invigorated, sustained, and renewed with each new breath—quietly reveals itself in this simple autonomic function.

The rhythm and texture of breathing varies like everything else. Though the gentle issue and return of the breath from the body seems an endlessly repetitive circle, where each inhalation and exhalation are identical, when we pay close attention, we begin to notice subtle variations in the flow of our own breath. By settling the mind on it, we find that breathing is actually interesting and engaging to watch. It is our idea of breathing that is mundane, pedestrian, and boring. The actual act of breathing, as it is happening right now, can be endlessly fascinating.

- Find your actual breath as it moves right now beneath your nose.
- Settle your mind on the sensation of the breath as it moves in and out.

- Pay attention to natural fluctuations in the pattern of the breath—its slowness or quickness, shallowness or depth.
- The simple act of breathing keeps your body and mind alive.
- Let awareness of the breath fill your attention. See if you can be aware of the breath even as it disperses within and throughout your body.
- Try to notice where breathing ends and the rest of the body begins. You can feel that the entire body participates in breathing as blood carries the oxygen obtained in the lungs.
- The body breathes and can be felt as a scintillating energy.
- Approach this exercise with a child-like sense of fascination and enjoy the wonder of being able to breathe!

If the simple act of breathing can be captivating, then sitting in traffic or listening to a tedious story can be fascinating. Every moment of life conceals wonders and miracles if we allow our attention to settle below the superficial. Mindfulness opens the door to enchantment. We open that door by giving ourselves permission to be here, in this moment. We needn't rush headlong in relentless pursuit of the next bit of flash and sparkle to find our lives interesting. Letting go of Facebook, Twitter, and our smartphones to attend to the wonders of simply being, here and now, enriches our experience of life far more. Rather than turn on the television to stimulate and engage your thirst for engagement, sit for a while and engage the miracle that is your own life as it spools itself out along the ever unfurling and receding cycle of breaths. Fascinating!

Fear

Everyone fears something. I fear being considered to be incompetent, fatuous, or careless in my work as a therapist. More personally, I am afraid of being unloved, disliked, or rejected. It has been my

observation, both personally and professionally, that we are all generally afraid that our lives will not go according to plan. To make matters
worse, when things don't go according to plan we harbor a concom-
itant fear that the disappointment or shortcoming will diminish us.
Although we are in no real danger of physical harm or injury, fears like
these can nonetheless be paralyzing.

Fear arises from a mistaken apprehension of reality. The Buddha
called this mistaken apprehension "ignorance" or "delusion." We labor
under the erroneous belief that our well-being is contingent on circumstances: "If life is comfortable and I get what I want, I will be
happy. If I don't, I will be miserable." When we examine this assump-
tion more carefully, it doesn't hold up. We regularly see people who are
happy in spite of the terrible circumstances of their lives and others
who are hopelessly depressed even in the most ideal of circumstances.
It is our attitude toward the circumstances in which we find ourselves
that makes the difference.

The Buddha told us that we are liberated from fear when we stop
clinging to the mistaken idea that things are enduring and embrace
the reality that life is impermanent. When we stop struggling against
the continual change that unfolds, however imperceptibly, in each
moment, we are liberated. Of course, it is difficult to simply break the
habit of clinging to our ideas of how things ought to be or of how the
plan ought to unfold, but with practice we can weaken that habit and
replace it with a healthier one. Pushing and pulling against the way
things are may still happen, but each time it does provides us with
another opportunity to let go. When we learn to accept what comes,
we are freed up from our fear of things not being what we want them
to be. This freedom makes us more flexible and capable of adapting to
circumstances as they shift around us.

In my case, I tend to be more afraid of committing social errors that
will cause me shame than I am of something physically harmful happening to me. Indeed, I've ridden a motorcycle at 130 mph and I rou-
tinely fly down snow-covered mountains on a snowboard with skilled
abandon. I am always afraid that I will say the wrong thing, make the
wrong choice, or otherwise embarrass myself socially.

Once, for example, at the end of my workday I was feeling exhausted, so much so that I wondered if I might not be coming down with something. Not feeling entirely well, I was looking forward to going home and getting to bed early. As I left my office, I bumped into an acquaintance. He was heading to a new restaurant nearby to meet his wife and some friends, and he invited me to come along. I didn't want to go, but then my constant worry about making a bad impression socially kicked in: "If I say no, how will they interpret it? Will they think that it means that I feel they are not worth hanging out with? Or will they think that I am antisocial? Am I passing up a perfectly good opportunity to build relationships with them?" In the end I politely declined to join them and went home to rest. I was immediately beset with feelings of anxiety, imagining a cascading series of social consequences that would be the fall-out for refusing the invitation. This reaction led to a state that was not particularly restful.

Luckily, my practice of mindfulness came to the rescue. I took a few moments to sit, compose myself, and follow the breath. First, I had to identify what was happening—to give it a name and recognize it for what it was, a cognitive distortion. I was allowing my anxiety-gripped imagination to run rampant. Next, I noted the feelings produced by the downstream physical sensations of my fear, and spent a few moments breathing into them. This is just the feeling of anxiety playing out in the body—a fleeting physical sensation. These feelings have a half-life and will decay if we allow them to. In order to break the cycle of negative rumination, I reflected on my worries in a larger context—the results of passing up a chance to socialize, my social standing with friends, my career, and even my life will eventually end. This too shall pass. It isn't worth it to worry about such trivial things. I will feel better tomorrow and if I've offended in any way, I can always make amends. Taking care of yourself when sick is a responsible and understandable course of action. Your friends would want you to do so, too.

I did feel better the next day, having taken the rest that I needed. Later, when I ran into my acquaintance, I asked him about the dinner. He wasn't disappointed in me in the slightest. All my anxiety over it had been just a product of my fear-gripped imagination.

Flourishing

As a psychologist I tend to only meet clients when they have a problem. They're stressed out. They're hurting. They're confused, anxious, and depressed. Their relationships are falling apart. Rarely do I find myself sitting across from someone who feels happy with his life, and when I do, it usually means that he won't be needing my help for much longer.

As is natural for a discipline that grew from the wish to relieve suffering, the field of psychology has largely developed around the study and treatment of mental disorder, rather than around the study and maintenance of mental well-being. But as with our conceptions of medicine in general, we have begun to think about prevention as being of equal importance with treatment when it comes to thinking about well-being. The emergent field of positive psychology seeks to study and promote positive aspects of mental health. Martin Seligman, one of the founders of the field, cites five "pillars" of mental flourishing: positive emotions (such as happiness), engagement or flow (a concept similar to mindfulness), relationship, meaning, and accomplishment. For ease of discussion, these five are sometimes referred to by the acronym PERMA.

Although most of us would agree that these elements are important for feeling as though we are flourishing, the press of our everyday lives, filled as they are with work, errands, and other responsibilities, may lead us to overlook or forget them. Sometimes life can be so busy that we feel we need to just hunker down and try to get through the day. If we let this way of behaving become routine, we end up sleep deprived, feeling continually overwhelmed by everything on our to-do lists, and out of touch with the ourselves. In order to flourish, we need to break through the feeling that we need to rush off to the next thing, and take the time and effort to cultivate positive emotions, engagement, relationships, and so on. To do so, we will need to let go of our lists, for at least a little while, to attend a bit more to the present moment.

The practice of mindfulness can be incredibly helpful in this regard. By creating a little calm in an otherwise mentally busy day, we give ourselves the opportunity to attend to how we are in the present moment. Are we latching on to and elaborating negative emotions? Are there positive emotions we might focus on and cultivate instead? Resting the mind on the breath and settling into the moment will help us reflect on such issues. When we see that we've fallen into negatively elaborating on our experiences, we can use our practice of mindfulness to cognitively reassess the reality of things. We can also use our practice to attend to what is good in our lives and to cultivate a sense of gratitude with relation to positive elements we may have overlooked. The more we cultivate such thoughts on the cushion, the more likely they will be to come to mind while we are amid the rush of the day. The sitting session may yield positive emotions and is, itself, the experience of engagement. After having sat, we have accomplished something and the practice may be part of a larger meaning system of training the mind in the service of awareness. Sit with your spouse, a friend, or a community and you have also enhanced your relationships. Just by doing some meditation practice, you can engage all five pillars of PERMA.

His Holiness the Dalai Lama is a great reminder of the possibility of living in the world with positivity. Despite the great hardship that has befallen his people, being exiled from his homeland, seeing his religion and culture decimated, and the slow progress with gaining freedom and civil rights for Tibetans inside of Tibet, most of the time he smiles a genuine smile and seems very happy. Rather than getting caught up in negative thinking about what has happened or is happening, he keeps intimately in touch with his positive emotions and doesn't lose sight of their value. His Holiness is never far from laughter, regardless of the circumstances. And his laughter is infectious: his own flourishing causes those around him to flourish, however little.

Working on developing positive mental factors requires effort, but suffering involves a lot of effort as well. We have simply become habituated to the negative ways of thinking and feeling that perpetuate our unhappiness. So it's really a question of where we want to use our energy. Smiling takes less energy than yelling, and the more we smile the less we want to yell. Flourishing is a skill and like any skill it can be practiced. The more we practice the pillars of mental flourishing, the more refined, robust, and available our well-being becomes.

Flow

I am sitting, as I write this chapter, in a stuffed chair at the farmhouse of the Barre Center for Buddhist Studies. I have been typing away on my laptop as a small workshop takes place in the next room. I feel fully engaged with what I'm doing; things seem to flow without effort. Falling into the groove of writing gives me a profound sense of enjoyment. Conditions are just right—the task is challenging without being overwhelming—I am in *flow*.

Psychologist Mihaly Csikszentmihalyi developed the concept of "flow" to describe the interaction between challenge and skill level for a particular task. If our skill level for a particular task is low and the challenge that the task presents is also low, for example, we are likely to feel apathetic: "I might as well not get out of bed." If we have a moderate level of skill but the challenge presented by the task is still quite low, we are likely to feel bored with the task. And if our skill level is high and the challenge of the task is still low, we are likely to feel relaxed: "This will be a piece of cake." On the other hand, if level of skill at a particular task is low but the challenge of the task is high, it is a recipe for anxiety. If we were to pit our moderate skill level against a highly challenging task, we are likely to feel aroused. But we only get into flow when there is a good fit between our skill level and the challenge of the task.

In some senses, the notion of flow captures the immersion aspect of mindfulness: time disappears as we become absorbed in the practice of attending to now; our sense of self also evaporates. A robust practice of mindfulness can also help to facilitate flow, even when engaged in some other task, like writing. This happens because when we develop mindfulness in practice, we find that the state of mindfulness spills over into those parts of our life when we are not on the cushion. Activities that might have been characterized as skill-less or boring, like washing the dishes, when practiced with mindfulness can become challenging enough to produce a sense of flow. Maintaining the quality of our attention—its energetic, interested joy—can actually be challenging enough and require enough skill to get us into the flow.

Mindfulness similarly works at the other end of the spectrum, too, by altering the experience of what would otherwise be overwhelming. A task at work that regularly produces anxiety, such as completing an important project and presenting it to one's peers, may provide an opportunity to experience flow if approached with mindfulness. Mindfulness allows us to notice, in a detached, observational way, anxious sensations in the body and to move our attention away from building narratives of "I can't do this" around them. Mindfulness helpfully separates the anxiety narrative from the bodily sensations that underlie them. The space that this move opens allows us to focus on engaging with the task at hand. The endless applicability of mindfulness can transform any task into an opportunity for flow.

Our meditation practice, itself, can lead to states of flow. The practice of meditation itself is a way of schooling the mind to be engaged with what is happening—even something as simple as breathing in and out. When the sense of "doing" meditation drops away, we enter into flow. When we encounter the present moment without story, commentary, or complaint, flow won't be far behind.

Focus

When I was a young child in the mid-1960s, I was a precocious mover. When I was as young as three weeks, my mother reports that I would flip over on my own. When she reported this behavior to the pediatrician he didn't believe her. Then I did it in his office. I would not sit still as a young child. I learned to walk late because I didn't have the patience for it. I was happy crawling and, apparently, I was quite skilled at it. I was constantly on the go exploring my environment, opening drawers, lifting things up looking for who knows what. At night, I wouldn't sleep. My parents resorted to packing me in the car where the hum and motion proved hypnotic. When I was three or four the pediatrician wanted to put me on Ritalin. My parents refused. It's ironic that I would become a mindfulness meditation yogi. I confront this restless legacy every time I sit to meditate. Often, my body does not want to sit still; all too frequently my mind does not want to sit still either. Practice for me involves a lot of returning to now rather than staying solidly situated in my object of concentration.

Focus, like any psychological faculty, varies from person to person. Some have exceptional focus, some have poor focus, while the great majority of us will be somewhere in the middle. Unless you are one of the relatively rare few who have an exceptional ability to focus, focusing attention is a skill that needs to be developed through practice. Without my practice of meditation, my focus would be far worse than it is. With practice, however, I am able to focus my mind. It's not natural for me, but it is a skill that I have consciously developed over thirty years of different kinds of meditation practice. I can't claim to always be perfectly focused, but at times my mind does become completely still and those moments are wonderful.

I find that developing focus requires effort, patience, and consent. It takes effort to retrieve attention from fantasy and return it to reality. Even if we manage to pull ourselves out of our fantasies, we are likely, at first, to slip back into them without really noticing. We have to learn to be patient with ourselves in order to make a practice out of dwelling in the reality of the here and now. Lastly, we may need to give ourselves permission to focus. Allowing ourselves to abandon habitual fantasy opens up the space in which we can sit with an experience long enough to really get to know it—in our pores, our bones, right into the very center of ourselves.

Diffusion of focus keeps us from experiencing life in a deeper way. Spreading our attention out is likely a natural way of keeping track of our superficial environment, thereby keeping ourselves safe. But spreading our attention thinly, keeping it constantly occupied with distraction and entertainment, also keeps us from really getting to know ourselves. If we rest our focus on just one thing, we quickly notice our own growing restlessness, impatience, and boredom. It's hard to sit still for long: the mind grows impatient and wants fresh stimulation.

Restlessness, impatience, and boredom are obstacles to perfecting our practice, and focus is their antidote. We encounter these obstacles when we focus, but they can be deconstructed one by one. "Restlessness" is the conceptual label that we apply to the physical experience of certain energies in the body. The same is true of impatience and boredom. Just as the mind constructs these experiences around bodily sensations of energy, mindful focus can deconstruct and release them.

Try this experiment at work where, with all of the demands on our attention, diffusion of focus is the norm:

- Begin by spending five minutes focusing on your breath as you breathe naturally.
- Give yourself permission to focus on a single task for a period of time.
- Turn off your instant messaging system, close your email program, and turn off your smartphone for this period.
- Give your complete attention to the task at hand. If your mind is restless and wanders, gently return your focus to the task, working in this way until the task is complete.
- When you feel restless, impatient, or bored, allow yourself to simply let your attention settle into focusing on the task at hand.
- When you have completed a task, turn your attention to the next task, and continue working through your day.

See what it feels like to be fully engaged in each task. You may find that you are more productive. Focusing like this is mindfulness in action. With more mindfulness practice, it will be easier to focus. The flawlessness of practice is not a perfectionist ideal of what should be but an embrace of what *is* in the moment. It's an opening to the perfection that is present in this moment—every moment.

FOMO (Fear of Missing Out)

I once led an early spring retreat in northern Vermont. Even though the winter had been mild and we had already had a week of summer-like weather in March, when we are usually still buried in snow, the arrival of what felt like genuinely spring weather in April was a cause for celebration. It was sunny and mild; the wind wasn't blowing harshly out of the northwest as it had been for the past couple of weeks. But I had committed myself to leading a meditation retreat, an activity that required that I remain inside all day. As I sat with the group of retreatants, a storyline developed in my mind: I was "missing out" on the sunshine. "I could be playing golf this afternoon," it said. A subtle nagging feeling crept along in the wake of this story, a feeling of being deprived. I was caught up in the "fear of missing out" (FOMO).

FOMO seems to define a lot of our contemporary anxieties. "Keeping up with the Joneses" used to mean having a preoccupation with materialism, but nowadays our sense of missing out seems to be tied as much to the quality of our life experiences as it is to material wealth. Fear of missing out ties our sense of well-being to our ability to collect new experiences. We begin to feel as if other people are having a better time than we are, that whatever it is we're doing, there is something more fun or rewarding going on elsewhere. Our fear of missing out creates a sense of restlessness that compels us to incessantly seek satisfaction through new stimulation. In the worst cases we are reduced to seeking stimulation just for the sake of stimulation. The seventeenth century French mathematician and philosopher Blaise Pascal anticipated FOMO when he wrote, "All men's miseries derive from not being able to sit in a quiet room alone."

Social media seems to feed our fear of missing out and causes it to grow. Now we don't have to imagine what everyone else is doing, we can see it right there on our Facebook feed. This may explain why people spend so much time following their social media feeds and why Twitter, Facebook, and other social media are so popular. Here is "life" streaming before us in real time. Sometimes the stream acts as a tool to help organize protests in Iran or bring donations to earthquake ravaged Haiti, but it is equally as likely to tell us what our "friends" ate for breakfast, where they went on vacation, or how cute and intelligent their children are. For many of us, the strange, voyeuristic phenomenon of social media ends up being a tool with which to measure and judge the quality of our own lives and experiences; a tool that lets us see just how much we are missing out on.

Mindfulness is powerful medicine for the relief of our fear of missing out. When I began to be drawn into the fear of missing out on a beautiful sunny day while leading the retreat, I took that feeling into my practice in order to investigate it. First, I acknowledged the presence of FOMO—an easy enough step given how insistent the feeling was. I then had a choice: I could continue to build my narrative of missing out or I could redirect my attention to what was actually happening at the moment. Fear of missing out, like any other product of the mind, arises, vies for attention, and eventually fades away if touched with awareness. So I touched it with awareness: "Ah, there is FOMO. Now back to the breath." A few moments later, "Ah, there it is again. Back to the breath. The sun streaming through the windows of the studio feels warm. I have that to enjoy."

Like any other narrative, the fear of missing out can be very compelling when it begs for attention; it can draw us into fantasy and make us feel bad about ourselves. Applying a bit of mindfulness helps us to appreciate the reality of who we are and to develop a confident self-sufficiency that is immune to the constant comparisons with others that come with FOMO. There is plenty in this very moment that is worthwhile. We needn't compare it to an imagined something *else*. It is unlikely that we will miss out on life if we remember that each moment—no matter what is happening—is complete in itself, provided we give it our full attention.

Forgiveness

I was attending an annual conference sponsored by the Center for Mindfulness, "Healthcare and Society." One evening I arrived in a rush, late to the dinner gala. When I entered the ballroom I saw that things had already begun as everyone was already seated at their dinner tables. I dropped my bag on the edge of the room and hurried to the vacant buffet table. I thought that I was so late that everyone else had gotten their food and sat down already! As I was about to help myself to dinner, one of the staff approached me: "I'm sorry sir, we haven't started serving dinner yet." I was in such a rush that I had not observed that the other four hundred or so mindfulness practitioners, educators, researchers, and clinicians were not eating at their tables but had been waiting for dinnertime to begin. It was too late; my presence at the buffet table sparked a run on the dinner line. The staff relented and everyone helped themselves to the meal.

While I was slightly amused at my sudden hero status for "liberating" the hungry masses, I was mortified by my lack of mindfulness. I felt embarrassed that I had acted so mindlessly in front of the crème de la crème of the mindfulness community. I began to feel a bit disappointed in myself. In the end, I had a choice: I could castigate myself for rushing in carelessly and without paying attention or I could forgive myself and let it go. Knowing how damaging it can be to hold on to anger, even toward oneself, I let it go—a teachable moment, like all mistakes.

Failing to forgive is bad for our health. Holding on to grievances, whether toward someone else or ourselves, can lead to chronic stress. Holding on to stories about how we were wronged is like ingesting poison—it festers and corrodes our health and happiness.

We may fear that letting go of our sense of being wronged will diminish us in some way, but the evidence tells us that we will be better off if we are able to forgive. Being vulnerable can be scary. Practicing forgiveness requires that we are confident enough in ourselves to know that letting go of past hurts is not an admission that others are right to harm us, or that we deserved it. Forgiveness is about not letting the past dictate how we feel in the present. It is an act of letting go of the narrative of victimhood and coming to live in the present moment.

Forgiveness may involve actually forgiving someone, but it can also be a personal process of acceptance that doesn't involve another party. Those we forgive may be long dead or we could forgive an institution, or god, or life itself. We forgive whoever or whatever it is that we feel has harmed us or wronged us.

Our practice of mindfulness is quite useful when it comes to forgiveness, because it helps us to disengage from destructive narratives of grievance. Our practice can help us to see how we build our identity as the aggrieved party by clinging to the story of what was done to us. Mindfulness helps us to more clearly see the difference between what happened in the past and what is happening right now. According to Sam Standard, a forgiveness expert, mindfulness can be the basis for cognitive restructuring, because it allows us to see how harshly we judge others and to notice the physical tension we carry when we can't forgive them.

Here is a short practice for applying mindfulness to the act of forgiveness:

- Scan your mind to settle on the hurt that you feel has gone unresolved, whether it's a slight, an injury, or a general disappointment with yourself or another.
- Find the location of the unresolved feeling in your body.
- Bring your attention to rest on the physical sensation. Breathe into it.
- Note how the story of grievance drives the feeling of being wronged. These two aspects—the story of being wronged

and the physical sensation of being hurt—compel one another.

- Continue to breathe into the feeling of hurt, and touch the story of that hurt with awareness, recognize it for what it is—a story—and return your attention to the breath.
- Follow the breath, gently returning yourself to watch it ebb and flow each time the story calls you away.
- Practice until you feel the sense of being wronged relax out of your body and the demand of the story fade.

Mindfulness allows us to use each breath to open our hearts and minds to forgiveness. Learning to forgive not only lifts the burden of black thoughts from our minds, it relieves much of the unhealthy physical side effects of the stress that follows in their wake.

Generosity

Generosity, or *dana*, is the virtue of giving our time, money, and energy to something other than ourselves. In Buddhism generosity is the practice of selfless giving. The Buddha taught generosity as an antidote to greed. The Buddha offered his teaching without fees and gave people the opportunity to practice generosity by giving whatever they felt comfortable to give in return. Traditional Buddhist temples in Asia do not charge audience members to hear teachings or to attend services, but rather subsist on whatever their congregants offer. In America, many Buddhist centers also charge nothing for teaching and charge only minimal fees to members to cover expenses for room and board during retreats.

For my part, I was clinically trained in Mindfulness-Based Stress Reduction. That training consisted of therapeutic courses for which fees were charged. I myself conducted such courses for years and also taught other types of mindfulness workshops where I collected money. When I moved to a new office space with a larger meditation studio in 2010, I had the chance to revisit the type of fee-structure I would use for providing meditation instruction. I was finally in a position where I felt I could offer meditation without charge in the new space. Because I felt the wish, naturally from my own side, to offer my instruction, I was able to practice the generosity of giving it away. I could finally recognize the opportunity to practice generosity and it felt very good to follow through.

Look out for the small opportunities to practice generosity in your life: put a quarter in an expired parking meter, give someone your seat on a crowded subway, pick up your spouse's socks without telling him or her and without expecting a thanks in return. Commit small random and anonymous acts of kindness toward others. See how it feels to give a little of yourself.

From small acts of sharing you can gradually work toward larger ones. When we have a generous spirit it is hard to get caught up in narratives of what we lack in life. We can even think of practicing mindfulness as an act of generosity toward ourselves. Practice itself is a gift of time and energy—give it to yourself!

Goodness

Whether humans are fundamentally bad or good is a perennial subject of debate. Some, like Freud, say that we are by nature bad—we tend to be selfish and self-serving—and it is only society that impels us to be civilized. Others, like the Buddha, say that we are by nature good and that whether our goodness shows depends on how we conduct ourselves. It is easy to watch the evening news and feel as if the world is filled with nothing but people who behave selfishly. But listening only to the evening news can be very misleading, as the great majority of human life that goes on peacefully each day doesn't make the news. The truth is that our potential goodness is really what we make of it.

Psychological research by Peggy Mason and her colleagues (published in *Science*) has found that even rats—who share a similar basic emotional brain architecture with other mammals, like humans, for example—show a basic goodness in their behavior toward their fellow rats. In one study, two rats spent time living together getting to know one another. Then one of the rats was removed from the common living space and placed in a confining tube where it was in distress. Its previous roommate would paw, bite, and do whatever he could until he managed to trigger an escape mechanism that would free his "friend." Researchers noticed that one rat would work to free the other even if the other would still end up separately sequestered in another cage. Their actions seemed to be inspired by a desire to help, perhaps even altruistically. In further experiments, researchers demonstrated that the helpful behavior was as strong as food-seeking behavior. When presented with the task of retrieving an attractive chocolate treat, which competed for the rat's attention with the task of freeing up his "friend", the rat would do both tasks. The rat did not gobble up the chocolate and then unfetter his friend, but took the chocolate and shared it.

Studies like this support the Buddha's insight that goodness is part of who we are as sentient beings. To practice goodness means to not promulgate greed, hatred, and confusion as we move through the world. Be nice. Help other people. Don't add to the suffering of the world. Don't commit violence, even in the privacy of the mind. Over time, each individual kind act, each moment of nonviolence, helps to bring out the natural good that exists within us.

Mindfulness helps us to *be* good. According to the *abhidamma*—the technical literature of Buddhism—mindfulness is not just giving our full attention to whatever is happening in this moment; it also means giving our attention without hatred and without greed. Mindfulness, in this literature, is associated with "beautiful states of mind," including absence of hatred and greed, faith, a private and public sense of respect for that which makes us gentle, and a sense of equanimity. With mindfulness comes tranquility, lightness, malleability, proficiency, and rectitude. From this standpoint, mindfulness is not just a means of honing attention, mindfulness is ethical: it is goodness embodied. When we are mindful, we attend closely to our actions and guide them toward the beneficial. When we are mindful, we reveal our inherent goodness.

Grace

One day I was walking by the pond near my home. It was stick season in Vermont. The trees were bare and winter couldn't be far away. But it was near sixty degrees. I was walking with my neighbor's dog, listening to some groovy music (mindfully of course; and the day before I led a mindfulness of music retreat). As the friendly breeze greeted me, my arms extended and I felt like I was flying. This is grace. I was happy and sad at the same time, feeling the poignancy of my own dog's death earlier this year, enjoying this exceptional day, this exceptional moment.

Take a moment to find your breath as it moves through your body. Breathing is miraculous. With the simple act of breathing, a bit of the world flows into and out of us. Our breathing bodies are connected to the much larger whole that is our universe. We breathe in air warmed by the sun and cooled by the night winds. When we look up at the night sky on a clear evening, the twinkling starlight we see is hundreds, perhaps over a thousand, years old. As humans, we are newborns in the face of universal time. But as bodies composed of "star stuff," we are part of something much more than the stories we tell of ourselves. Our existence, while small and seemingly inconsequential in the grand scale of things, also bears an enormity beyond words. Grace touches us when we pause to consider the inexpressible vastness of our lives.

Grace is always waiting here within us; we don't have to manufacture it. We just have to get out of the way. Grace reflects our inmost nature: it emerges when we let go of hope, fear, doubt, and regret—when we settle into the moment at hand. When we are lost in regrets about the past or hopes for the future, we fail to appreciate the reality of what we are *now*. Our incessant storytelling obscures the grace of the present moment. Regret, fear, excitement, and annoyance keep us from enjoying the simplicity of now.

The practice of mindfulness can help us to move through the world with grace, rather than being buffeted by continuous emotional spasms. It helps us to cultivate a sense of being touched by love, awe, and connection. Whether we believe that grace is given by God or that it is simply a natural part of ourselves, being mindful can put us in touch with grace. Grace is available whenever we can suspend our internal, storytelling mind.

Whether we are devout believers or atheists, grace is a gift that is available to us as soon as our mental tensions are relaxed. Learning to be mindful brings grace into our lives. This happens regardless of our religious beliefs, practices, or history. If we can let go of the running stories in our minds, grace will reveal itself. If we can stop pushing and pulling against reality, this very moment will become grace. We are already connected, complete, and content: nothing needs to be added; nothing needs to be taken away.

Gratitude

Before they eat, Buddhists take a moment to acknowledge the contribution of the countless beings that have made their meal possible, from the worms that aerate the soil, to the farmers, pickers, truckers, and grocery store clerks that touched the individual ingredients that end up on their tables; even life forms as small as bacteria play a role in the successful production of our food. This simple act of acknowledgment imbues us with a sense of gratitude for what we are about to eat and keeps us from taking the food that sustains us for granted.

It is possible to pass through our entire lives without ever noticing the sense of entitlement that comes with having plenty. Sometimes we may even get caught up in thoughts that ruminate on what we don't have or on those things in life that just don't go our way. But even those moments in life when things don't go as we'd like them to are something to be grateful for. Each disappointment in life is like a little bell, ringing to awaken us from the daydream of what could be and to alert us to the facts of what is—reality. Everything is changing all the time and in ways that we can neither predict or control. In time, the possessions that we have will break or wear out, opportunities will fade, and things will pass us by. Eventually even our bodies will break down. So it behooves us to be grateful for our mobility, health, and everything else while we have it. Gratitude helps to awaken us to the wealth that we possess in this very moment. Gratitude prevents us from sleepwalking through life.

True gratitude takes nothing for granted. It's amazing that we can even do the simplest things that we do. To breathe, to walk, to think, speak, and love is nothing short of marvelous. I've recently injured my knee. I sometimes complain to myself about how I can't do everything that I used to be able to do. To relieve myself of this unpleasant mindset, I've taken to enumerating all the things that I have to be grateful for. Once I reflect with gratitude on what I still have that I take for granted, I also feel grateful for the injury itself. Without it, I might not have taken the time to realize how much I have to feel grateful for.

In order to cultivate a general sense of gratitude, it is useful to begin keeping a list of things for which you are grateful:

- Begin by listing the things you are thankful for in your life.
- Keep your list handy so you can refer to it when you are feeling dejected, discouraged, or dispirited.
- Not everything on the list needs to be unique to your own life; some may be generic to the human condition, even the fact that we exist at all.
- Make your list a living document by regularly adding to it. This will help you to notice more things to be grateful for and, of course, will make the list longer!

It becomes harder to take life for granted when we curate such a list. You can also use the list as a motivational tool at the beginning of a meditation session. Every day—indeed, every moment—that we have is a precious opportunity.

Greed

"Disturb the peace with the awkward brilliance of the Rondo sandal," the ad said. French made, little patent wedge, open toe, dog-collar strap around the ankle. "For six hundred dollars in a perfect size seven, they could be mine," said Rita, one of the members of my meditation community. She yearned for these shoes: "They would make me everything I wasn't. Young. Sexy. Desirable. They would show off my thin calves, my best feature. My hips were expanding, boobs drooping, face wrinkling. My husband hadn't made love to me in months. But the shoes would change everything."

Rita was captured by the fire of desire, passion—flat-out greed. She was consumed with wanting an object and all the "benefits" she imagined these shoes would confer. She decided to talk about the desire for these shoes with the meditation community before making the purchase. She could not afford the shoes right away. So I encouraged her to meditate on the feelings of desire to see what might happen to them. I invited her to consider that they might be impermanent like everything else.

It seems clear that the continuous pursuit of material comfort does not bring happiness. The richest 17 percent of the world's population uses 80 percent of its resources. Yet studies show that personal happiness does not continue to increase forever along with increased wealth. Our perceived satisfaction flattens out after reaching a certain level of material comfort. In other words, the continued accumulation of wealth, of material, doesn't necessarily make us any happier. Eventually, the pursuit of satisfaction through accumulating things becomes futile because it only encourages more desire: the more we have, the more we want. When we look outside of ourselves for fulfillment in objects, experiences, and status, we get caught in the trap of greed.

Greed is not just the overt taking of too much or not sharing with others. Greed can be a more subtle process of desire, one in which we find ourselves reaching out for things all the time: "I want this; I have to have this." Over time our insatiability grows to pervade our lives until relentless wanting, consumption, and, ultimately, unhappiness become the norm.

Even our own spiritual practice can be tinged by greed. As we develop skill at meditation, for example, we may find ourselves wanting to hold on to the blissful states that arise during a session. By clinging to the pleasure of serenity, we may lose sight of the purpose of the practice itself: to lessen our clinging to fleeting experience. Buddhism and many other spiritual paths consider preoccupation with rarified experiences to be a pitfall or trap. We must not lose sight of the fact that experiences, including those had deep in meditation, are impermanent by nature. Otherwise, we may simply be replacing attachment to gross material objects with attachment to fine mental states. While pursuing spiritual practice, greed can slip in the back door. Spiritual materialism can be just as destructive as garden-variety materialism. So we must always be vigilant against greed.

Subtle forms of greed may be at work anytime. It is easier to recognize when we find ourselves resisting or fighting to preserve our experience against change. Over the course of our meditation training, we have plenty of opportunities to practice letting go of this type of greed:

- Eventually, you will without a doubt reach the point of practice where you are not ready to end the session when the time allotted for the session has elapsed. The feeling is something like not wanting to turn off the showerhead after you've finished bathing: you'd just like the pleasant experience to continue.
- Recognize this mindset as a subtle form of clinging to experience. Just the fact of recognizing it loosens it a bit.
- Shift your focus from the pleasantness of the experience to its fleeting nature. The breath, with its cyclical rhythm moving in and out, makes a good anchor for attending to change.
- Keep your attention focused on the fleeting nature of the experience as you end the meditation session and move from the period of practice back into your daily routine.

Practice in this way each time you encounter clinging to meditative experience. Over time, you will develop a sense of detached equanimity with regard to such experiences, allowing them to come and go without provoking greed. The technique of recognizing clinging, shifting focus away from the pleasant quality of the object of clinging to its fleeting nature, and then, with clear awareness, letting go of the object of clinging can be used both with overt and subtle forms of greed. There is nothing wrong with having pleasant experiences. But when we cling to them with greed, the things we enjoy quickly become poison. Sometimes to truly appreciate what is good in life, we have to learn to let it go.

Hope

My father died of lung cancer, a slow, difficult, and uncertain illness. I had hoped that he'd reach out to me for help (since helping people cope with chronic and serious illness is what I do professionally). Each time I grasped on to that hope, I became disheartened. My job, rather, was to keep showing up, available to him if needed, without imposing my agenda of hope onto him. He never did reach out for help in coping with his condition. We also never had my hoped-for reconciliation or final reckoning of our relationship before he died.

Hope is the wish for an imagined positive future outcome. When I say, "I hope things will be different," I am simply wishing that things will somehow be better than they are now. But, as much as I'd like it to be otherwise, a simple wish does not make things happen. While the hoped-for change may be possible, it won't be probable unless I take an active role in making it happen. Sometimes "hope" is used as synonym for optimism. But optimism usually coincides with personal effort: I have taken steps to make it so, therefore I am optimistic that it will be so. Hope, on the other hand, is a fantasy about the future with little standing in the present moment.

From the perspective of mindfulness, hope and fear develop when we lose touch with the reality of the present—when we fantasize about the future and dwell on the past, respectively. One of the benefits of cultivating mindfulness is that it roots us firmly in the present moment. A good deal of the fantasy that preoccupies the undisciplined mind falls by the wayside. We begin to see more clearly the paths of action that will build our future, see more clearly our current capabilities, and begin working where we are in order to develop the skills needed in order to realize our goals.

Before we become mindful of our own thoughts and fantasies, we may not even realize how hope has been holding us back. Hope, with its idealized image of the future, is an attractive emotion. It appeals to a pure, childlike wishfulness deep within that most of us have lost touch with by the time we are adults. In the sense that it presents an idealized version of the future to work toward hope is not all bad. The campaign slogan of the 2008 Obama campaign, "HOPE," spoke deeply to the American people, disillusioned after nearly eight years of war and the economic hardship it brought home. But we all learned that hope alone doesn't get things done. Hope for the Obama presidency was realized, but it quickly became clear that there remains a huge amount of real-world work to be done before anyone can feel optimistic about the future.

As counterintuitive as it sounds, we must let go of hope in order to achieve our hopes. Until we can see ourselves honestly, here and now, and understand the steps that we must take to move forward, hope is just wishful thinking. And where there is hope, its old partner fear is never far behind. If we can let go of hope and fear, even when we stumble, we will not falter in our task, whether it is working to better ourselves or to better our world. So the next time you find the fantasy of hope creeping in, invite yourself to let it go; leave the old, frustrating pattern behind and embrace the freedom that comes with being here, now.

Impermanence

I feel great. All of my aches and pains are quiet. My mood is good. The weather is perfect. My belly is satisfied, neither hungry nor too full. I feel connected, creative, and confident. It feels great to be alive! But how long will it last before an ache arises, hunger reappears, my mood changes, and the rainclouds mass once again?

The only certainty is uncertainty. Impermanence is a universal law. Things are constantly changing. The Buddha didn't claim to be the first to notice this fact, but he did make it a central point of his teaching. He taught that if we fail to understand impermanence, we are bound to suffer. This is so because, although the world is in flux, we treat it as if it is stable: when things go well we forget that they will eventually end, and when they go poorly we think that they will remain that way forever. Our inability to grasp the fleeting nature of an experience makes us miserable, whether the experience is coming or going.

Our greatest blind spot with regard to the changing nature of things is ourselves. When I think of myself, I tend to think of "me" as something that remains unchanging in some essential way. Of course, I recognize some variations—hunger, sleepiness, aging, etc.—yet there is something that is *essentially me* that remains constant. The Buddha saw through this illusion. He saw that there is no "me" outside of the ever-fluctuating instances of experience that comprise "me" in any given moment. In other words, "I" am really just an idea pasted onto all the different processes that go into my experience of being "me"—

thoughts, feelings, perceptions, and actions. Thinking of myself as a stable, unchanging person is a recipe for frustration, misery, and disaster.

Bringing a bit of mindfulness to the way we perceive ourselves can help relieve many of the expectations and disappointments that come from habitually thinking of ourselves as static. With consistent practice we begin to notice more regularly how things are always changing. Impermanence isn't an abstract concept; with a little attention we can observe it directly. Practice can help us to accept variation in ourselves—our moods, ability, and performance—as natural. Whether we rise to a challenge or stumble along the way, it is all a part of the ever-changing intricate dance of now. Whether things are going perfectly our way or we feel down or ill, we will more easily remember that "this too shall pass." It shall pass because *everything does*.

There was an incident with the FedEx delivery man the other day. One of my dogs got aggressive toward him. I had been in the shower when he came to the door and I could hear the dogs barking. I rushed down to catch him before he left, but in letting him know that I was here I opened the door and let the dogs out. There was no biting, but the guy was shaken up. I felt awful, dreadful, and consumed with regret for my mindless stupidity. As these feelings arose, I touched them with an understanding of impermanence. "This too shall pass" can feel like a cliché but the lived experience confirms that it is true. I did all that I could do in the moment. I made my apologies and made the mental note never to do that again. I knew that the intense emotions of guilt and self-reproach, indeed all emotions, have a half-life. They decay. I would feel better the next day and the next day after that. If I left the storyline that gave rise to feelings alone and paid attention to the energies in my body, that decay would be expedited. Of course, I had to register the "teachable moment" from this situation, and beyond that it did not require thought; impermanence would take care of the rest.

Knowing impermanence helps us to deal with adversity and it also keeps us from growing attached to the status quo. We learn to meet circumstances where they are and deal with them as they are, rather than attempting to shape them to our expectations. Being able to let go and embrace the moment, come what may, is the path to peace.

Integrity

Integrity has two meanings: it can mean being a person of integrity—moral, ethical, of honest character—and it can also mean "intact." When we practice mindfulness we embody both aspects of integrity: we are upright and whole.

Mindfulness is the translation of the Pali word *sati,* which means "to remember." When we are mindful we remember ourselves as capable of being conscious, intentional beings. We look below the superficially frantic, habitual, and stressed out mindset with which we typically conduct our lives, to put ourselves back together. We use the body scan technique to bring all of the parts of our bodies back into balance with one another, and to balance our bodies with our minds. When we are intact and whole in this way, we are in a better position to act as ethical beings in the world. We will be less likely to unwittingly harm others or ourselves when awake to the pain that such actions can cause.

Integrity stems from being good and being good stems from integrity. The more we practice mindfulness, the more this reciprocal relationship is strengthened. I aim to be good, not because I want to be well liked or to conform to some abstract moral principle, but because I know that is the best way to live my life. Good intentions reduce the amount of dissatisfaction, anguish, and suffering I have to contend with.

We can discover the benefits of integrity in our own experiences. Lying, stealing, and being violent require energy in the moment and have downstream consequences, and that energy could be better spent in other places. This sense of being whole feels better than having holes in our emotions and relationships. Mindfulness fills these holes, brings us to one piece—a wholeness that comes from being aware of what is occurring in our bodies from moment to moment, understanding how our emotions give rise to actions, and participating in our relationships rather than using them as a proving ground for acting out every petty impulse, old fear, and irritation we have.

Integrity describes the practice of mindfulness itself. Instead of getting lost in the random parade of thoughts, images, and emotions that usually accompany our moment-to-moment experience, we gently direct our focus onto the moment itself, and settle in it, just as it is. Although random thoughts or feelings naturally bubble up in the mind, by remaining stably settled in the moment as it is, we can experience this busyness of our minds without judgment. When we stop judging the chatter of our minds, we can finally let go of the constant pushing and pulling against its activity. Stable, long-lasting mindfulness comes from observing the activity of the mind with a light touch.

We can be ethical with ourselves. Instead of beating ourselves up with harsh, punitive thoughts, we can just allow our imperfections to be as they are. With practice, we will develop the sensitivity to know what actions will and won't be in our best interests. Witnessing thoughts and feelings as they come and go helps us to understand them as insubstantial and passing, rather than engaging them as substantive enemies of our inner calm. Why get angry at clouds in the sky for their passing shadows?

Intention

I am sitting in what will be the first of many appointments this day. It's going to be a long day with little opportunity for rest or reflection. My work as a psychotherapist is to be present, to listen, and to advise. A key component of this effort is to know that I am breathing and to stay connected to this breathing throughout the day. My intention is to make breath awareness a constant companion throughout my day. By attending to breathing and the body this breathing is situated within, I come into the present moment without the distractions of my storytelling mind. I listen through my body; I talk through my body. My heart opens and becomes spacious—able to take on anything that arises. I begin my work with the intention of being present and my breathing keeps me there.

Intention is an important mental factor that accompanies every waking moment. It moves us toward objects of perception and plants the seed of future action. Intention asks the question, "What is my aim here?" Attention, a close relative of intention, keeps us focused on that aim as we work toward it. If we don't bring awareness to what we are doing in the moment, we will be pushed hither and thither by conditions. Having a firm intention, setting clearly defined aims for our practice, helps us to keep our attention on task.

Setting one's intention is a crucial part of developing a robust practice. Learning to establish a clear intention prior to leaping into an activity also carries over into our daily lives off the cushion. In general, it is useful to understand the intended aims of what we do, and to carry out our actions with a purpose in mind. Much of the time, we end up running on autopilot, moving from one errand to the next without much thought or awareness of what we are up to. Cultivating the practice of establishing intention is an effective way to bring our minds more in line with our actions.

With regard to the daily practice of meditation, we establish our intention as follows:

- Once you have seated yourself in a comfortable and stable meditation posture, spend a few moments reflecting on the purpose of the session you are about to undertake.
- It may be that you've noticed that your mind is frequently carried away by a worry or lost in storytelling and you want to develop mindfulness in order to have better control of your mind. Or it may be that you feel that mental turmoil

makes you less present for friends and loved ones and you want to improve your sensitivity to others in order to better respond to their needs. Spend a few moments reflecting on what has brought you to pursue the practice of mindfulness.

- With your motive clearly in mind, set your intention by resolving to take up the practice for the allotted session. You should develop a strong sense of commitment to the practice at this time.

- As you work through the session, each time distraction carries you away from the breath, reaffirm your intention as you gently return attention to the breath.

- When the allotted time for the session has run out, end your practice by reaffirming your intention to cultivate mindfulness to achieve your goals.

Regularly reaffirming our intention is a good way to generalize our practice in our lives off of the cushion. With an ongoing commitment to practice, you can also embrace the intention I described above to relate to others through a solid grounding of awareness in your breathing body. Working to maintain intentions is also an effective way to transform moments of distraction into opportunities for practice. When we find that we've been mindlessly going about our business, taking a moment to remember our intention brings us right back into our ongoing practice of mindfulness. When we lose sight of our intentions, we end up rudderless, pushed along by conditions. Being aware of our intentions will help to create harmony between our actions and aims.

Interdependence

No one is truly an island in this world. Even if we were the world's biggest loner, living off the grid, we would still be a part of the interdependent web of being. We just can't breathe without the trees exchanging carbon dioxide for oxygen. We just can't eat or drink without the crops that grow from the earth and the water that runs in the rivers. We wouldn't even exist if not for our mothers and fathers. Yet we may become so caught up in what we have and don't have that we lose sight of our interconnection with everything and everyone else on the planet.

The food that we eat would not be available without interdependence. Such a great number of living things contribute in some way to each meal we eat. If we include the unseen microbes that aerate and prepare the soil, that number becomes countless. And then there is the rain that provides the moisture that makes up 90 percent of the mass of plants and 75 percent of the mass of animals. Without trees, there wouldn't even be an atmosphere. Every morsel of food we eat requires the interconnected efforts of many beings in an expansive web of life.

Interdependence applies not only to our relationship with the rest of the world, it applies to our private experience of the world as well. All subjective experiences are interdependent. Thinking depends on feeling, which in turn depends on perception. Perception depends on contact of sense organs and sense data. The selection of sense data on which to focus depends on intention and motivation. Knowledge of the objects that we perceive in the world depends on our paying attention to them.

If my motivation is informed by stories of want, such as "I need those new golf clubs," I will begin to produce particular thoughts associated with the object of my desire. "I will be really happy once I have those clubs," "I might even be able to get significantly under par!" and "How can I keep on playing with these crappy old clubs?" The more these types of thoughts come up, the more I feel as if I'm losing out on something. The feeling of losing out will touch off memories of past instances of the same. Soon thought, emotion, and memory weave a full-fledged narrative to justify my desire: "I've missed out on enough in life! I deserve these clubs!" If I finally break down and buy the clubs, I get a few moments of joy out of having attained the object of my desire. But soon their novelty fades, and my mind begins chasing some other object: "Maybe a new pair of golf shoes is what I need?"

Understanding the interdependency of desires allows us to intervene and redirect them. The patterns of our thought inform the patterns of our behavioral habits. Rather than focusing on what we want or what we lack, we can choose to simply focus on the moment at hand. Thoughts that let go of desire and feelings of lack produce a sense of equanimity in the mind. Thoughts of contentment and feelings of equanimity touch off memories of feeling satisfied with life as it is. Soon these positive thoughts, emotions, and memories work together to replace narratives of want and desire with narratives of fullness and contentment.

Understanding the interdependent nature of the world and our experiences of it allows us to see the rich potential for change within each moment.

Intimacy

We can think of mindfulness practice as the process of becoming intimate with something—like reality in this moment, like what it feels like to be alive in this moment. Intimacy requires us to pay attention. In order to know something or someone, we need to actually be present with it or them.

Intimacy could be thought of as the process of realizing how little we actually experience what we think we do—the places, people, and things in our lives as they unfold moment by moment. The poet David Whyte warns that a relationship must "keep the edges of the unknown alive" lest it become deadened, stagnant, predictable. Similarly, Gabriel Garcia Marquez said of his wife, Mercedes, "I know her so well now that I have not the slightest idea who she really is." Realizing how little we experience of what we experience is the entry point to intimacy.

Consider looking at a work of art. Actually take an afternoon to go to your local museum to sit with beautiful works of art, to spend time taking in the richness of a single work.

- Settle yourself before the painting or sculpture, sitting or standing as you prefer or as is available.
- Take a moment to focus your mind on your breath, following it as it moves in and out, until the mind becomes quiet and centered in the moment.
- Now, look at the work of art, allowing your eyes to slowly roam over its features, sometimes seeing it as whole, sometimes taking its individual elements.
- If thoughts such as "I like this part" or "This color isn't as pleasing" appear, simply note them and return your attention to the naked elements of the work of art itself.
- The better you are able to leave off the expectant aspects of thought, the more you are likely to be surprised by the piece.
- Continue for as long as you like.

This type of looking is a form of meditation. Looking at things again and again, particularly those things that we think we already know, helps us to become aware of how much is in fact obscured by the feeling that we already know it. It is a common function of human cognition to quickly label and categorize the numerous pieces of sensory data that flood our senses at any given moment. Most of the time this function is useful: it helps us to quickly make sense of the world we encounter from day to day. We don't need to re-meet each and every person, taking their uniqueness in any given moment into account, in order to negotiate our daily interactions.

However, we may sometimes lean too heavily on the categories and labels our minds assign to experiences in the world. This can be particularly detrimental when it comes to relationships with others, as we begin to see people as more and more static. The truth is that we are all changing all the time. To be truly intimate with someone is to allow for that change, to open ourselves to the endless possibility that each person represents.

Joy

Just look at a baby—laughing, smiling, playing. Or look at dogs doing what they love to do—romping, chasing, nuzzling for affection. Joy is natural.

So why is it so difficult to feel genuinely joyful? Because we are afraid. Fear is an obstacle to joy. Fear includes big-ticket items such as threats to safety, job security, relationship challenges, and so on, but it also includes the general fear that things won't go our way, that we might not live up to expectations, or that our lives just won't amount to much. Fear obscures our natural tendency to feel joy.

To get more joy out of our lives, we need to let go of our ever-present fears and anxieties. Mindfulness can be a reliable method for doing this.

- Take a moment or two to settle the mind, letting your attention gently come to rest on your breath as it moves in and out.
- Once you have become suitably present with yourself, make a quick survey of the various subtle fears that you carry with you. You needn't judge yourself for harboring fears; it's quite normal that fears build up like a joy-concealing crust over time.
- Simply note the fears, and breathe in their heaviness.
- As you breath out, imagine that you are letting go of your fears, choosing instead to be here in the moment.

■ Continue for as long as you like, setting a firm conviction to leave fear behind in your daily life as you end your session.

Letting go of fear is just the beginning to really finding joy in life. When you feel that you have left fear behind for the moment, do something you really love, something that brings you true joy. Play with your pet, spend time with your children, or sing a song from the bottom of your heart at the top of your lungs. Even better, share your joy with a friend or loved one! As we set aside storytelling, we begin to experience things as they are and get more in touch with the innate sense of joy that comes with being alive.

Judgment

Some of the clients I work with in my practice are very judgmental about their own thoughts. They find some of their thoughts to be evidence of weakness, stupidity, or triviality. Sometimes unwanted thoughts arise in the mind involuntarily. Thoughts that we would rather not have are not a sign of some moral defect but are simply the byproducts of the complex workings of our constantly busy minds. We may not even be conscious of most of the thousands of thoughts we have every day, and we almost immediately forget many of those that we are aware of having had. Out of that vast crowd of thoughts, a few may be mean, dark, or bizarre.

Although sometimes judgment can be helpful, many times it is not. Good judgment helps us to distinguish right from wrong and is a basis for skillful action. Bad judgment, on the other hand, is a knee-jerk reaction rather than a thoughtful response. When judgment runs out of control, we hastily condemn others and berate ourselves for the things we've done. No one likes to be around a judgmental person.

Learning to accept ourselves, both good and bad, helps us to have a more balanced and honest self-assessment, and to be a little more generous with our judgment of others as well. We all think or do things that might surprise us. Thoughts about sex, money, or doing something inappropriate might pop into our heads at the most inopportune moment. The sudden intrusion of unwanted thoughts, particularly when we are trying to focus on virtue or selfless practice, can be quite jarring. But the truth is that our minds run on autopilot like this most of the time. It is the very context of our sitting practice that highlights the automatic, intrusive, and even bizarre nature of our thoughts. In a way, the meditation context has given you the opportunity to be aware that this type of thought occurs.

The key to facing the ugly underbelly of our own thoughts is to learn to withhold judgment. Instead, we can learn to relate to mindless thoughts in a healthier way. When unwanted thoughts appear during meditation, choose to look at them in any of the following ways:

- Simply recognize these thoughts for what they are: the seemingly random firing of neural networks in the brain.
- Place the thoughts in context: all humans have such thoughts; they are the natural chatter of an untrained mind (and to some extent continue even when the mind is trained).
- See intrusive thoughts as an opportunity to be mindful: recognize distraction and undisciplined mental activity, and practice a gentle return.
- Remind yourself that you are not your thoughts and return your attention to the breath. Repeat as necessary.

Rather than extending the influence of unwanted thoughts, we can diffuse them by learning to accept that they occur and simply moving our minds onto healthier objects. And developing a more balanced assessment of ourselves allows us to learn to be less judgmental of others. Little by little, our practice of mindfulness helps us to shed the aspects of our mental life that deprive us of peace and happiness.

Karma

Generally we think of karma as "What goes around comes around." But karma has a simpler meaning in Sanskrit, the language from which it is drawn: *karma* means "action." In Buddhist writing, karma is rarely treated alone but is paired with another term, *phala*, which means "fruit." Thus, the Buddhist concept of karma is really the notion of actions and their fruits. The idea points to the simple truth that our actions have consequences. This is what Buddhists mean when they talk about "karma."

The Buddha taught that karma hinges on intention—the thoughts, feelings, and aims that motivate our behavior. This way of thinking about karma pushes us to look behind actions to consider the mental states that lead us to do them. From one point of view, we can say that the idea of karma compels us to pay closer attention to the thoughts, feelings, and aims that drive what we do. Yes, looking at karma superficially, we can say that killing or stealing will lead to unpleasant consequences—we may be caught and punished, or we ourselves may end up being killed or stolen from. But looking more deeply at the motives that drive those acts, we can also say that murderous thoughts or unbridled covetousness prime us to think other similarly unwholesome thoughts. The more we grow accustomed to thinking in this way, the more likely it becomes that we follow up on our thoughts in action. Behavior in turn reinforces thoughts and feelings. Before long, we are swallowed up in a seemingly inescapable morass of habitual thought and action.

This is, in fact, how the Buddha characterized human existence. Like driftwood on a stormy sea, we are tossed about in life by our karma and mental afflictions. Mindfulness practice gives us the clarity of mind to see the currents at work beneath our own thoughts and behavior. By slowing down and seeing ourselves more clearly, we become able to actually do something about our karma.

For instance, when thoughts of anger or bitterness appear—"I can't believe he said that to me! I'll show him next time!"—our habit is to be drawn into self-serving narratives and to reinforce or rationalize our motives for acting angrily toward the object of our dislike. Our thoughts, feelings, and aims collude to perpetuate our bad karma with respect to that particular person. Bringing mindfulness of thought and feeling to bear on the situation, we can see that this sort of thinking will bear only the fruit of more bitterness and anger. Recognizing the workings of karma allows us to choose to see things in a different way. It may be that the disrespect or insult of another prompts our own bitter narrative, but aren't they equally subject to their own karma? It may be that they unthinkingly act badly because they are also tossed about by their own afflicted habits of thought. Understanding the working of karma offers us the opportunity to choose a different course of action.

Every action has a consequence. This is true even of mental actions, such as thoughts and feelings. Looking at our behavior and the behavior of others as consequences of the thoughts, feelings, and aims that motivate them disarms the sting of insults, the allure of attractive goods, or the disappointment with the thoughtlessness of others. Armed with greater sensitivity to our own motives and intentions, we can choose the type of seeds we sow and look forward to sweeter fruits.

Landscape

Hiking during Vermont's mud season can be quite a challenge. Thick pools of mud and puddles of water lay scattered throughout the trail. If I step in the puddles, my feet will get wet and my toes are sure to ooze with mud. Wanting to avoid the mess, I am tempted make a path around the puddle. If I do this, the wet, muddy "wound" in the trail grows larger, making it take longer for the trail to recover. Walking around the edges of the puddles just makes them larger and makes the damage last longer. At a trail near my home, hikers are urged to walk right through the middle of the puddles in order to help the trail heal.

Likewise, we may be tempted to skirt around the muddier spots in the landscapes of our own lives. But we merely prolong difficult situations by trying to avoid dealing with them. It is better to face them head on and make our way through them. As our ongoing practice of mindfulness allows us to survey the landscape of our lives and our minds, we might consider practice to be a sort of exploration. Like intrepid pioneering mapmakers, our job is not to look only at those areas that seem inviting but to make an exhaustive and honest record of the lay of the land. Sometimes this includes tromping through bitter brambles or trudging through inhospitable swamps.

Sometimes we find that we don't want to face ourselves in the moment. Thinking about tomorrow or reviewing yesterday, telling ourselves stories about how we'll be different later—we'll do anything but face ourselves as we are now. This is like clinging to the memory of a sunset seen from a beautiful vista as one wades through a mosquito-infested bog. It may be difficult to deal with the hardships we face, but just like the bog, they are a natural part of the landscapes of our lives. Swamps and bogs don't draw the vacation crowds, but we know that these muddy locations are a vital element in the health of our ecosphere. The troubles we must all face in life are just the same: none of us wants to go through them, but when we have faced them, made it through, and pause to look back, we realize that even great adversity has something valuable to contribute.

As our natural mindfulness grows with practice, we grow a little more capable of approaching troubles with interest. Like explorers, mindfulness practice embraces a spirit of adventure. No matter how dark or dangerous the territory may seem, a spirit of inquiry can keep you engaged with your practice. A healthy sense of mindfulness helps us to keep our cool, while appreciating the various changes in the landscape, whether pleasant or unpleasant, as we make our way down the road.

Happy trails to you!

Legacy Reflex

What arises in consciousness is not necessarily our fault. What we do once it arises is, however, our responsibility. Many people who have experienced trauma, for example, will experience sudden memories of the trauma when triggered by something that reminds them of it. Such memories are automatic responses, which I call "legacy reflexes." Memories of trauma may appear shortly after the trauma or years later. I worked in the mid-'90s with World War II veterans who had been troubled by a sudden resurgence of traumatic memories fifty years after they had originally occurred. In those cases, it seemed that the major life change of retirement precipitated many of those memories.

Every time the traumatic material presents itself to the mind we have an opportunity to work through the memory and the emotions that accompany it. Without a clear sense of mindfulness, however, our default mode of dealing with troubling experiences may work against our recovery. If we slip into self-criticism or frustration because we feel we ought to be "over it," the energy of the trauma is likely to remain intact and may even grow stronger. If, on the other hand, we step back and observe the traumatic memory objectively, keeping our emotional responses in check, then the energy of the traumatic memory will weaken.

Most traumas come along with a heavy narrative: I served in battle with my buddies, some of whom didn't make it back; I grew up in a family where someone abused me; just when I needed my parents the most, they split up. These types of stories become a part of the legacy reflex associated with the trauma. Consequently, we easily fall back into these narratives when traumatic memories are retriggered. Being able to remain dispassionate, looking at our traumatic memories as just mental events rising and falling in the mind, forces a bit of a gap between the trigger and the ensuing reflex. Opening this chink in the causal chain of trigger, reflex, regret, self-blame, and so on, allows us to take control of how our traumatic memories will play out.

When faced with traumatic memories, try the following:

- Take an interest in the memory, as if you are a dispassionate observer encountering it as an object of interest.
- As much as you may feel the urge to fall into the narrative associated with the memory, or to push the memory away, resist, and continue observing it *as* a memory.
- Rather than thinking, "Why is this happening to me?" think, "This is just something that happens."
- Let go of guilt, judgment, or blame in relation to the memory.

Developing a robust sense of mindfulness helps us to create a space between emotional triggers and legacy reflexes. Being able to see ourselves dispassionately and to approach our experiences with interest allows us to move beyond reflexive action, to reclaim our lives, and to heal our long-carried hurts.

Liberation

I just walked to my mailbox to put in some mail. My mind is circling around my to-do lists, turning over a problem, and paying attention to my recently acquired rescue dog running around in the yard. As I walk back to the house, I notice the trees that surround it. It is approaching peak foliage. At first, I see a flat, almost two-dimensional image of a once green tree now ablaze in an orange-yellow hue. It stands out as its neighbors cling to the green remembrance of summer. When I set aside all my internal chatter, this two-dimensional image becomes three-dimensional. I see it with more clarity. The colors become brighter, more enjoyable. I also notice how it sets against the profound blue of the morning sky. What was, a moment before, just another "fall tree" is now a rich experience. By coming into the now, I am able to see this tree more clearly—real and pure. I am liberated from distraction. My meditation practice helps me to get closer but my experience is still filtered through language, learning, and mood. I am closer to liberation and not quite there. Seeing the trees was a glimpse of the protean energies that give rise to my perceptions.

In Buddhist thought, "liberation" refers to the final freedom from all unskillful attitudes and action. We encounter the freedom that is natural to us when we stop pushing and pulling against experience. The poet David Whyte describes enlightenment as the search for safety—a place where the world cannot reach you. For him, liberation is attained through vulnerability. Liberation is not the quest to become inviolate. Rather, it is the openness that has relinquished "I," "me," and "mine." We only engage life freely, without fear and with great contentment, when we have stopped the mind's obsessive grasping. Where there is no grasping, suffering fades. Freedom from suffering is liberation.

Liberation doesn't mean transcending the mundane here and now to reach some ultimate realm. It can be found in the simple perception of a tree. The idea of liberation relates to our minds and the way that they interact with the world we live in. We are not free when our mind ties us up in ideas of what we do or don't deserve and how much better or worse off we are than others. Liberation doesn't mean that we wink out of existence or levitate above the clouds into heaven. Liberation means that we let go of clinging to things as being this or that, and take them exactly as they are. When we finally reach a state of peace with the moment and whatever occurs in it, we are liberated.

Our daily practice of mindfulness, no matter how meager it may be, helps us work slowly toward liberation. As the mind quiets down during meditation, we experience moments in which thought altogether ceases. The mind stops pushing and pulling and comes to rest in the now. The more we practice, the more frequently these moments come and the longer they may last. These short tastes of liberation are something we can carry with us into our day.

As our practice progresses, we begin to recognize when we are shoving and tugging against experience. Recognition is key to being able to let go sooner and with greater ease. If we can be mindful with respect to how we engage with our experiences even off the cushion, we can begin to make inroads against mental bondage. It is a simple process of progressively working toward our own eventual release. Each session of meditation helps us to build toward that goal.

To think of liberation as a far away transcendental ideal is a disservice to the immediacy of Buddha's teaching. We don't find liberation somewhere else, far away, but reveal it within ourselves by letting go of ourselves. The idealization of liberation as some form of mystical transcendence is an obstacle on the way. Who needs that pressure? Relax. You don't need to live your life sublimely. Just be as you are. Try not to add anything to the experience. Rest in the now—often.

Loving-Kindness

Buddhism retains a very strong tradition of deliberately opening our hearts to others. This practice is called "loving-kindness" or *metta* in Pali. It is interesting to note that the traditional practice of cultivating loving-kindness can either begin or end by focusing on ourselves. Either way, a core element of the practice is to cultivate feelings of loving-kindness for ourselves, too. Of course, it isn't healthy to develop narcissistic feelings of self-love, but neither is it healthy to live with feelings of unworthiness. The reason that Buddhists include cultivating loving-kindness for ourselves in the practice is because we can't very well love others if we don't love ourselves. True loving-kindness is indiscriminate and holds nothing in reserve.

I like to practice loving-kindness as an ancillary or supplemental practice to mindfulness. If I spend a few minutes raising a warm feeling of love prior to my meditation session, I find that my practice goes much smoother. I tend to have a healthier attitude toward myself when I get distracted, and toward others if they interrupt me. A typical session of loving-kindness meditation unfolds as follows:

- Begin by regarding yourself: here you are, a human being on planet earth (one of billions), this many years under your belt (just a few in the cosmic scope of things), and still finding your way in the wide world. While you may have good and bad traits, you are not all bad, and at least you are here working on becoming better. We are all doing our best to make our way through our lives, and we all equally hope for happiness and hope to avoid unhappiness. In this sense, we have some worth as simple beings looking to live our lives well.

- When you have developed a sense of positive regard for yourself, open your heart to send wishes for health, safety, happiness, and ease.

- Orally or mentally recite:
  May I be safe and protected from all inner and outer harm.
  May I have peace and happiness.
  May I be healthy and strong.
  May I live in the world with joy and ease.
- After cultivating loving-kindness for yourself, turn your attention to a friend or loved one. Gradually bring to mind all of those for whom you have a great deal of love—whether they are dead or still living, human or animal.
- Open your heart to them and wish them well just as you have done for yourself.
- Next, bring to mind a stranger, someone toward whom your feelings are generally neutral. Gradually expand your image of this stranger to include the great mass of beings unknown to you.
- Again, open your heart to these beings and wish them well.
- Now imagine a person with whom you feel estranged, angry, or bitter. Gradually expand the image to include all of those whom you feel to be enemies.
- Remember, they, too, are just other living beings who have found themselves in this world without knowing where they come from or why they are here. They too wish to be happy and hope to avoid pain.
- Open your heart and extend to them the same loving well wishes.
- When you have opened your heart to each group of beings and wished them well, settle your mind in this feeling of loving-kindness, and keep it in mind as you move on to your practice of mindfulness, or go back to the routine of your daily life.

It may be difficult to extend love to those who we feel have harmed us. We may feel that they don't deserve it. But this practice isn't about whether love is deserved or not. We work to cultivate loving-kindness because it is good for others and also because it is good for us. The more we cultivate love, the less our hearts have room to harbor hate. Being able to forgive those who have hurt us is the beginning of our own healing process.

Loving-kindness is a great balm for the emotionally wounded, and it brings a great deal of warmth to our practice of mindfulness. It helps us to see the sameness between ourselves and others, which in turn helps us to treat others as we would wish to be treated. Looking at the world with loving-kindness is such a simple practice. But its effects can be far-reaching and profound.

Meditation

Meditation may not be what you think it is. When most people hear the word "meditation" they imagine a yogini sitting in the lotus posture with a look of serene countenance, her mind empty of thoughts, tranquil, and removed from the world. This is one image of meditation that I was infatuated with and pursued in my youth. When I was twenty-two years old, I sat in the full lotus posture on a deerskin resting on a marble floor in an Indian ashram. I was seeking the neela bindu in my mind's eye—a scintillating field of blue light. When it was present I felt bliss, when it was absent I felt frustrated, disappointed, and deficient as a yogi. My meditation had an agenda—reaching particular states of bliss, affection, and transcendence. This was not mindfulness meditation because mindfulness meditation proceeds without such an agenda (or at least those are the instructions).

But if we become stuck on this simple caricature we will miss the true profundity of meditation. Meditation is not exotic, and it needn't even be confined to a cushion. We can meditate anywhere, given suitable inner conditions. When we really understand meditation, we understand that it is actually one of the most ordinary and practical activities in the world. The various meditative techniques passed down in the tradition are meant to contribute to the overarching project of weeding out bad mental habits and unwholesome behavior, and cultivating positive mental qualities and beneficial behavior in their place. At the end of the day, the purpose of mindfulness meditation is to facilitate insight. The meditation itself is not an end but a means to waking up to the nature of things. Understanding the nature of things is in turn a tool that helps us to let go of our own self-involvement in order to lessen personal affliction and negative behavior. Meditation, in other words, greases the wheels on the way to awakening.

Meditation is a practice that, like ballroom dancing, woodworking, or gardening, takes time to learn and develop a degree of skill in. You won't be an expert yogi the first time you sit for a session. But that isn't the point of practicing meditation. We practice meditation as a means of cultivating ourselves, as a means of refining the balance of healthy and unhealthy thoughts and behaviors within ourselves. Although we may have a notion of the perfection to be attained at the end of the line, this isn't really the overwhelming motive for practice for most day-to-day meditators. We practice without much thought of reaching the end because we feel rewarded by each step along the way. As we cultivate ourselves we grow more sensitive to our mental life and more capable of choosing how our experience will unfold from moment to moment. The beneficial changes that a regular practice of meditation brings are good for us and for those around us. There is something very satisfying about that.

If you are getting serious about pursuing meditation, there are a number of things that you can do to build and enhance your practice.

- Devote some of your home's real estate to it. Set aside a corner of your living space, or a spare room if you have one, which you can keep solely for your practice. Having a space dedicated solely to meditation is useful, because it allows you to avoid cues for other, less constructive behaviors, like watching television or surfing the Internet. A good meditation corner or room will also act as an inspiration to practice.

- Get the appropriate gear to make practice easier. A good cushion is essential if you plan to regularly sit. There are special cushions called *zabuton* and *zafu* that provide cushion for your knees and lift the pelvis up a bit to relieve stress on the hip as you sit. You can find these cushions online or at retailers in most places. It is good to keep in mind, however, that great meditation gear won't do the practice for you.

- Find a group to practice with. Meditation groups can be a great source of support for practice. And sharing the practice with others helps us to keep up our commitment to it.

- Eventually you will want to seek out a well-qualified teacher. There are many qualified secular and traditional Buddhist teachers in the world nowadays. Find a teacher that suits you and with whom you feel comfortable. A good teacher will help you find depths in practice that you did not know were there. They can also be wonderful guides along the way.

- When you have developed some skill at sitting for longer periods, you may want to pursue a retreat. A long meditation once a year can really recharge your batteries and boost your practice for months to come.

The key to developing a good meditation practice is to take it slow and steady. No matter how short your sessions may be, the important thing is to do it regularly. Just remember: whatever you do, just keep it up!

Mind

Buddhists enumerate six, rather than five, senses. According to Buddhist accounts, our senses operate through our eyes, ears, nose, tongue, body, and mind. The first five senses transduce sensory stimuli from the outside world into information that we can experience within. The mind produces thoughts, which are also transduced in a way out of the stream of prior experience. All of our senses are impersonal and simply function as a part of our natural makeup. The mind, just like our senses of sight or sound, operates much of the time of its own accord.

There is no one steering this mind. We don't own the mind and the mind is not who we are, even though our identity seems to reside there. The mind is an ever-flowing process, much of which happens outside of our awareness. Somehow consciousness arises out of this ceaseless flow of energy and information. Neither philosopher nor neuroscientist can tell us exactly what consciousness is. The mind is complex, powerful, and mostly hidden from our view. There is no little version of you residing in the mind pulling levers and pushing buttons, like the Wizard of Oz, to make the show go. Our sense of identity emerges out of these mysterious processes. When we don't try to own this flow, we can be in a state of peace. When we mistakenly have the sense that we stand apart from it, that peace is disturbed. It's not *your* mind. It's *the* mind. Mindful attention can help you operate this mind to the best of its abilities.

Among the fifty-two varieties of mental state that Buddhists enumerate there appear two that are very important in the practice of mindfulness: *vitakka*, or "directing the mind," and *vicara*, or "sustained mental engagement." Directing the mind is a mental state in which we actively choose to direct or redirect our attention. When the mind wanders from the breath during a session of meditation, direction of the mind allows us to recognize this and bring it back to its meditation object. Sustained mental engagement is the state of mind that settles well on its object of focus. This mental state is what allows us to focus continually on the breath when meditating. We rely on directing the mind to correct distraction and on sustained mental engagement to keep the mind in place. Directing the mind is another way to think about the "gentle return."

Generally speaking, the Buddhist idea of the mind is much more dynamic than the concept of a single unified entity. The mind is multifaceted and ever changing. The more we get to know its various states and qualities through meditation, the better handle we'll have on getting the mind to be our ally. When we practice mindfulness with this understanding of mind in mind, we can become proficient at directing and sustaining attention and enjoying the fruits of practice.

Mindfulness

Mindfulness has become a buzzword. You can see it everywhere—on the news, on the cover of *Time* magazine, and in different sectors of society such as healthcare, the military, education, and even the corporate world. You are implored to be in the present moment and this will help you to reduce your stress. Indeed, there is a growing body of scientific research showing mindfulness interventions may reduce stress as well as produce other beneficial effects.

In reaction to this popularity, some critics have dubbed this phenomenon "McMindfulness." They worry that mindfulness practices have been taken out of their ethical Buddhist context and have therefore been diluted. Despite these criticisms, it is hard to argue with the benefit these practices have brought to thousands of people. The expression of the Buddha's teachings as mindfulness in a secular context may just be the way Americans adopt the dharma, as has been done by all host cultures throughout history as the teachings of Buddhism moved to China, Tibet, Japan, Korea, and Southeast Asia.

Mindfulness practice in a secular setting can bring you to the dharma because it will bring you in contact with your mind and with that contact you'll have the opportunity to gain insights into the changing nature of things, the tinge of dissatisfaction that often accompanies moments, and a sense that you may not be running the show as you thought. I call this phenomenon "Trojan horse dharma." You start meditating to reduce your stress or to improve your focus at work and these wisdom benefits come along for the ride and may surprise you by popping out in your life.

It might be helpful to consider a scalable definition of mindfulness. Think of "mindfulness" and "Mindfulness." Mindfulness with a capital "M" is more than just attending to the present moment with nonjudgment. As described by Andrew Olendzki in his book *Unlimiting Mind,* the Abhidharma (ancient manuals of the Buddha's psychology) provides a more detailed definition of mindfulness.

Each moment of mind can move us in a wholesome or an unwholesome direction. Mindfulness is a wholesome or "beautiful" mental state. Mindfulness brings with it a retinue of other mental states such as confidence, conscience, equanimity, benevolence, absence of greed, and absence of hatred. The more we practice mindfulness, the more wholesome our minds become.

We may sit down to practice with a feeling of jealousy. Maybe someone else has the thing or situation you wish you had. This story is accompanied by negative feelings, filtered through other memories of jealousy, envy, and comparison. But once we engage mindfulness, we become aware of the feeling and the story that accompanies it. We're able to see these things as a choice, rather than being lost in them. Mindfulness helps us untangle our minds from the mass of unthinking narratives that we get lost in. A few moments of calm, mindful attention to our mental state, and the mind becomes beautiful.

When we take a serious interest in the practice of mindfulness meditation, we'll notice that the stance of being mindful is more than just paying attention without judgment. There are the other mental states that go along with mindfulness enumerated in the Abidharma. When we are present, we are not grasping after something; we pay attention without an agenda, so greed is undercut. We are likewise not pushing anything away in disgust, because we attend to experience without needing things to be a particular way. In this way, aversion is also undercut. We are open to what is. We are interested in what is happening, again, without any plan other than noticing what is present.

Mindful presence embodies a sense of confidence and disperses the typical anxiety and unease that often plagues the distracted mind. Little by little, mindfulness helps us to reform our baseline relationship with experience. In this natural state, we will be less inclined to act in ways that harm others or ourselves.

Meanwhile, when we are mindfully engaged with an experience, we feel a quality of lightness. Our mind is flexible, open, and tractable. These qualities can give rise to an abiding sense of peacefulness no matter what is happening. A great freedom is available in any moment we choose to be mindful. Mindfulness gives us the power, freedom, and the deep contentment that comes from being awake in the world.

Moderation

It's hard to really live awake if we frequently engage in extremes. This is absolutely true, but I have noticed that sometimes avoiding things we feel we shouldn't do can become its own kind of extreme. I generally do not eat refined sugar, but occasionally I will indulge in a red-velvet cupcake. To stick ruthlessly to my "no sugar" rule would itself be a bit extreme. Sometimes a cupcake is just the right thing. The trick to moderation is knowing how to balance indulgence and abstinence.

There is a saying among psychologists: "Don't should on yourself." "Shoulding on yourself" refers to clinging so stringently to personal rules that we feel miserable. Sometimes we can bend our rule and have a cupcake. When rules can be bent and when they had better be observed is relative to the particular context. In one situation, it may be prudent to abstain, whereas in another situation it may be prudent to indulge. It's always good to use moderation when it comes to treating ourselves strictly.

Whenever you say "I should" or "I shouldn't" you set up a boundary, an edge between the world and yourself. Conflict, tension, and anguish can arise from that edge and almost always do. Shoulds and the rules that underlie them provide a rubric to guide behavior. As such, they are a short cut in the decision-making process and become an easy way to avoid the existential challenges that we must face in each moment. When the rules are violated, as they eventually tend to be, recrimination may arise. In the beginning we may admonish and belittle ourselves, but before too long we find that we start holding others to our inflexible standards. Many of our own feelings of frustration, annoyance, disappointment, or anger with ourselves stem from breaking our own rules.

We all move through the world with an implicit rulebook. The more rules, the more opportunities there are to get in trouble. The more rigidly the rules are held to, the more woe. The Buddha issued a lot of decrees to his followers, which were eventually codified into the monastic code. For some the code became an inviolable set of rules that must be adhered to at all times, no matter what. Interestingly, when the Buddha lay dying, his disciples asked him which rules they should follow no matter what. In reply the Buddha said, "Keep those precepts that are most important, and use the others as needed." To some this may look like a rather vague and noncommittal answer. But I believe the Buddha knew what he was doing. His answer required intelligent reading of context and intent on the part of his followers. Essentially, he was saying, "Know when you should adhere to a rule, and know when you can leave it aside."

There is a traditional teaching story that highlights the need for flexibility. Two monks are walking along the road. As monks, they have taken vows of celibacy; they're not even supposed to touch a woman. They come upon a small river where a frail woman is waiting, not sure if she can cross. One of the monks picks her up and carries her across the water and then sets her down on the other side. The monks continue walking in silence and after a long while, the other monk says, "I can't believe that you touched that woman; it is forbidden." The rule-breaking monk simply replies, "I put her down miles ago; why are you still carrying her?"

When it comes to self-discipline, a good sense of moderation will help us to maintain a healthy relationship with ourselves. We're also more likely to make our friends happier if we can share a red-velvet cupcake with them from time to time.

Morality

Being good isn't just a potential ticket to heaven; it's a formula for having healthy relationships with our world and the people that live in it. We can just as easily look at ethics as a natural function of the biological as we can a set of "Thou shalts" and "Thou shalt nots." Humans naturally venerate goodness because it is beneficial to us. Respecting others and caring for the environment can help to keep our world safe and welcoming. Repaying kindnesses ensures a sense of value in doing things for others. We have the qualities of compassion, empathy, and love built into our DNA. In this sense, morality may be woven into the very fabric of the natural world.

Morality is the natural urge to find health and optimal well-being. Only in its most corrupted sense does morality become a cold system of taboos designed to ensure social control. The innate tendency toward morality is inextricably linked to our desire to be mentally healthy. We know, deep within ourselves, that our world would darken were we to utterly abandon care for the state of others.

Buddha was often likened to a physician, because the philosophy that he taught was said to bring mental and spiritual health. The Buddha's system is said to be a method for attaining well-being under any circumstance—even in the face of disappointment, loss, and misfortune. The method works because the key to well-being lies within us. From the Buddhist point of view, we act ethically, not because we fear punishment or it is expected of us, but because doing so actually makes us happy and diminishes our suffering. Caring for others requires letting go of ourselves. The more we think of our actions as they relate to others, the more our ceaseless clinging to ourselves wanes, and the hurt that comes with being fades.

The erroneous work of securing our "self" with little regard for others only leads to more misery. Most of the ills we see in our world can be traced back to selfishness in one way or another: war, pollution, and atrocities of all kinds have at their root the feeling that "I matter more than them." Morality, particularly the innate form of morality that every human possesses, is the great power that keeps these problems at bay and heals the wounds they leave.

Of course, when we are lost in self-important delusion and self-interested narratives, we may be blind to the way our own behavior affects the world we live in. A daily dose of mindfulness keeps the cobwebs of self-involvement cleared away, so our natural morality can shine through. In this way, to keep up a daily practice is actually to contribute our part to healing the world.

Nature

It's good to go back to our ancestral environment from time to time. While I love cities, I live in nature. I like to sit on my front porch and look at the trees swaying in the breeze, the stars shining bright in the dark Vermont sky, and the snow piling to several feet if it's a typical winter. I don't have to cross my legs into the lotus position; I just have to look, listen, and feel. Meditation seems to come more naturally in nature.

When you feel comfortable enough with your practice to experiment, you can try practicing in a natural setting. Walking meditation is one way in which this has traditionally been done.

- Walk slowly and pay attention to your breath and to the movements of your body.
- As you move through your surroundings, pay attention to the sights and sounds that appear.
- Slow your walk to a steady, even pace, so that you notice in greater detail the flora and fauna of that particular place.
- Keep your focus steadily on what you see, what you smell, or the sensations arising in your body as you walk.
- Rather than letting the mind wander from plant to plant, identifying one and then the next, simply take in the greenery nakedly as it is without conceptualization.
- Continue your meditative walk for as long as you like.

Practicing outside helps to break down the artificial separation we sometimes impose between "practice" and the rest of the world. Rather then feeling that we live in the world, as if it is a container that we occupy, we can begin to see ourselves as part and parcel with the world. The oxygen atoms that fill the atmosphere become a part of our bodies as we breath in the air, and the carbon dioxide that is our respiratory waste flows back into nature to feed the leaves as we exhale. Our own skin seems like a boundary, but in reality the elements of the nature that surrounds us are the very same elements that make up our flesh and bones. Getting out of doors to take our practice for a walk in the woods or open fields is a way of reminding ourselves that we and our world are a single whole.

Nature provides a ready vector for mindfulness practice. It isn't that mindfulness is impossible in an urban landscape, but noise and activity can be very distracting. Still, even landscapes undeniably altered by human populations cannot erase nature. And something about the nature that lives in the unfurling and receding of breath in the body preserves our feeling of connection with nature even when sealed up inside concrete walls. Prisoners serving time who take up the practice of meditation manage to find some connection with the serenity of nature with the slimmest of pickings available to them, perhaps a blade of grass poking through the asphalt. Of course awakening doesn't require living in a bucolic monastery, because we can awaken anywhere at any time, but fresh air and blue skies can nurture our spirit.

Nirvana

Nirvana is one of the most commonly misunderstood concepts in Buddhism. It literally means "blown out," as when the flame of a candle has been extinguished. Because of its usage in popular culture, nirvana is often imagined to be a transcendent reality—an ultimate existence that is more real than our ordinary lives. It is true that nirvana is a state quite different than our normal state of experience, but the idea has been blown somewhat out of proportion in popular culture. The Buddha chose the metaphorical term "nirvana" to describe his enlightenment, not as an otherworldly transcendent experience, but as the final extinction of the fires of suffering in himself.

When we lose our sense of perspective, we grow preoccupied with a desire for things to be a particular way. We crave things that bring us pleasure more and more, and we push away whatever brings us displeasure. We worry that our comfortable situation will change, despite the fact that change is inevitable. Struggling against reality generates dukkha. Our happiness and peace of mind are burning up in these blazes. The flames of attachment, hatred, and ignorance consume us in every moment.

Think about a bonfire. As long as we feed wood into the fire, it keeps burning. When we stop fueling the fire, it goes out. When we realize that everything is changing and there is no self to protect from the disappointments of not having what we want and having what we don't want, we are less beholden to desire. Stop feeding the fires of attachment, hatred, and ignorance, and they die out. When the fires go out, that is nirvana.

The fires of our passions may extinguish in any given moment, if only fleetingly. The fires cool a bit when we drop the narratives around "me" and we become mindful of the present moment itself without adding anything. Of course, we may fall back into self-centered narratives and the flames will be fanned back to life. But for those brief moments we taste nirvana.

Nirvana is not some mystical concept; it's right here, right now, whenever we can stop the mind's grasping after experiences, imposing conditions, and identifying with a self as if it weren't or shouldn't be changing. Nirvana is not some superior reality; it is this reality experienced without clinging to the self. Nirvana is special but not supernatural. Although practice and effort make it more likely that we will find nirvana, it is always present within us, waiting to be discovered at any moment. Nirvana is less a destination and more a readiness to let go.

Nirvana is possible when we relinquish all concepts—including the concept of nirvana.

Noble Eightfold Path

The Buddha taught that the path to release from suffering was comprised of eight interrelated disciplines, which he called the Noble Eightfold Path. The Noble Eightfold Path consists of Right View, Right Resolve, Right Speech, Right Action, Right Livelihood, Right Effort, Right Mindfulness, and Right Concentration. "Right," rather than referring to "right and wrong," refers to "wise" or "skillful" action. These eight disciplines can be grouped into three basic types—wisdom, ethics, and meditation—each of which supports the other. The idea of this eightfold path is that practicing its disciplines will lessen our suffering, increase our understanding of life and its meaning, and make us people better able to care for others with wisdom and compassion.

Tiger Woods is one of the most recognizable athletes in the world. In 2009, a sex scandal stained his public image, wrecked his marriage, and derailed his golf game. He lost endorsements and his habit of winning tournaments. At the time of his disgrace, he had been the world's number one golfer for over five years. It took him 923 days to win again and it took nearly two and one half years for him to regain his status as world number one. Tiger's improprieties and fall from grace are a good example of how these eight disciplines work together.

The scandal—where Tiger had indiscriminate affairs with multiple women—and the lies following the scandal are clear examples of lapses in Right Action and Right Speech. Speech is speaking the truth, of course, but it is also not gossiping, and avoiding idle chatter and harmful words. Right Action means not causing harm to others through our actions. Tiger's speech and action caused a lot of harm. He lied to his wife, he lied to the public, and he lied to himself. His actions had a negative impact on what was otherwise his Right Livelihood.

The scandal and its aftermath seemed to hurt his concentration. Without Right Action and Right Speech, Right Concentration is hard to muster—the preoccupied mind cannot rest easy. Without Right Concentration, Right Mindfulness is hard to pull off. Playing golf is difficult, unfathomably difficult at the professional level. There are many variables to attend to in any given moment. If negative karma has been stirred up by unskillful actions or intentions, it's hard to be mindful of what one needs to be mindful of while playing the game. Instead of attending to the myriad and subtle factors in the moment, the aftermath of unwise actions intrudes into the space of now.

We all struggle to find our way in the world, embracing the "rightness" of the Path. We all have places where we fall down. When we do fall down, we can contemplate the skillful action we can do right now to reestablish ourselves on the Path. The Eightfold Path is aspirational—a role model for how a buddha, an awakened one, would live. By living like a buddha, we become more like a buddha ourselves, come closer to realizing our awakened buddha nature. Buddhist scholar Damien Keown described the path like this: "The Eightfold Path is thus a path of self-transformation: an intellectual, emotional, and moral restructuring in which a person is reoriented from selfish, limited objectives toward a horizon of possibilities and opportunities for fulfillment." Such is a noble invitation.

Now

I was sitting in a group meditation during a course at the Barre Center for Buddhist Studies one morning. About halfway through the meditation the sound of an alarm clock began to issue from the dorm rooms below the meditation hall. My first thought upon encountering the sound was, "Oh, there is an alarm clock." The next thought elaborated on the first, "I guess someone decided to sleep in rather than go to meditation." Along with this thought came the expectation that the sound would momentarily cease. Acknowledging the sound, I returned to breath and body sensations. The sound persisted. "Perhaps someone forgot to turn off their alarm when they came to sit for meditation, so it's not going to stop," I thought. I started to grow annoyed, with the sound itself and with the person I imagined was responsible for it. "Way to go, buddy! You've ruined everyone's meditation!"

But it *is* happening. This was the new landscape of now. My mind went back to tending the breath. But my thinking mind was unusually insistent that morning. As the sound persisted, another thought arises: "It's probably the alarm clock of that really annoying guy." Now that the thought had been personalized, the emotional tone of nuisance increased. Noticing this uptick in irritation, I returned yet again to breath and body sensations. And so the process went. I moved from resistance to acceptance of now. When I resisted, I felt aggravation, dis-ease. When I accepted, I felt peace, ease, even joy in the simple pleasure of attending to the breath—even with the alarm sounding. I vacillated between ignorance and wisdom.

Comparing this moment to other moments gets in the way of simply experiencing this moment. Cataloging all the faults of this moment gets in the way simply living it. Imposing prerequisites for this moment gets in the way of being it. However, the entire concept of good, better, best disappears when we stop imposing an agenda onto what's happening now. Indeed, when we bring our full attention to this moment, the question of good, better, best is no longer relevant. This moment is as interesting as the previous one was and as the next one will be, no matter what's happening.

When we start to pay attention to how we usually conduct our moments, we might notice a lot of "if onlys." "If only it were a little warmer." "If only *she* were here." We put a lot of energy into orchestrating this moment, striving to get the conditions to be just so. The message becomes: if things are not perfect, then the moment is lost. However, mindful attention to the present moment can salvage it no matter the circumstances. Mindfulness author and blogger Elisha

Goldstein calls the operation of reclaiming the moment by paying attention to what is happening with curiosity "The Now Effect."

Wisdom recognizes there is no point in complaining about what is when we can't change it. The "problem" of the unattended alarm was constructed. I built it. I went out of my way to make it into an issue. The fact that I didn't want it to be there is what made it a problem. The fact that I didn't think it should be there is what made it an issue. When I let go of these expectations, I could rest back into the moment. And that now, as are most nows, was the best moment of my life. Now can be the greatest moment of your life when you pay attention to it with mindfulness. Now is, of course, the only moment of your life.

Can you make it the best moment?

Occupation

Some time ago, I brought my cat to the vet after she got into a nasty fight. After the first visit, I discovered the vet had missed that her tail was broken. On the second visit, the vet and I had a disagreement. I insisted this visit was not a new visit but a continuation of the first and thus should not incur another charge. Years before I had spent thousands of dollars at this clinic treating my greyhound with chemotherapy. This history lent an intensified emotional charge to my current position. We were deadlocked. When my attention resided in the storyline of how the vet was "taking advantage of me" and how he was being ungrateful for my previous patronage, my blood boiled. When these strong emotions began to arise, I disengaged from the storyline where I was "right" and focused on the sensations in my body. I located the intensity of that energy, mapped its spread and movement, and felt its temperature. A moment later, I was sucked back into the story and manufactured more distress. Then a moment later, with mindfulness, I returned to my body. The rubric of moving from story to body helped me to get through the situation.

The story to body rubric is available each time we practice. After we have quieted the mind in meditation and unveiled all the activity beneath the surface of awareness, we can fully occupy the body. The body will register the activity of the mind. When we are stressed from pushing and pulling against experience, we experience that stress as sensations in the body. When we experience strong emotions (or even subtle ones), we feel them in the body, too. The body is a rich source of information.

The goal of mindfulness practice is to move the mind away from the stories that drive emotional reactivity to the body itself. Attention is directed to the energy in the body that is constantly arising and passing away. The energy of emotions is neutral—neither good nor bad. The stories that generated this energy, however, can drive us crazy. When we pursue the stories, the emotions keep churning. If we're not careful, we can become blind with rage and move through the world in reckless ways.

Mindfulness practice can help us to recognize when the story has gripped the mind and to shift mid-sentence into the seething energy of the body, just as I did at the vet's. We can drop into the body and chart out the sensations that are present; we can map them with interest. Suffering requires a story; misery needs a narrative. When we drop the story, relief follows. When the storyline surges back a moment later, we repeat the process.

Of course, if you try to do this for the first time in the midst of anger, you're not likely to be successful. It helps if you practice at times when things are relatively calm and to practice on a regular basis. This way, when something happens and you find these emotions arising, you have the skill to extricate yourself. It can also be helpful to work with less intense emotions.

- Right now, pause and notice the sensations that are in your body.
- Locate any particular patterns—notice their movement, sense of pressure, and any feeling of temperature.
- When you pay attention to the physical features of the sensations, you occupy the body with equanimity—a calmness that abides what is happening with an even-eyed attention, neither hating nor loving what is going on.

- You can look upon the energy with curiosity. "This is interesting."
- When the story drops away, the sense of "me" drops away too, and there is nothing for suffering to grab hold of. You are just with an event that is happening now.

Occupying the body also works with less intense situations, too. If you find yourself sleepy, hungry, or uncomfortable in any way, the same process of occupation can take place. The body is a constant register of what is happening. The body scan practice can help you monitor the body and use it as a refuge.

Openness

I did my graduate work in Buffalo, New York. Prior to starting school, I'd never been to that part of the country. On my first visit, a friend insisted that we go see Niagara Falls in his single engine plane. I thought to myself, "How cliché, I don't want to spend my afternoon at a tourist trap." However, I couldn't resist the airplane. My first view of this natural wonder of the world came from above. My previous closed attitude began to open as I observed, mouth agape, the features of the landscape below. As cliché as the falls had become, they were still magnificent—massive movements of water. The Canadian "Horseshoe" span of the falls moves six hundred thousand gallons of water per second! Because I set aside my preconceptions, I never tired of visiting the falls after my aerial initiation. Because I was open, each visit was wonderment, awe, and inspiration, regardless of the commercial development that abounded.

Openness is one of our fundamental ways of being—a basic feature of personality. People vary as to how open they are to experience both internal and external. Internal openness is nonjudgmental, allowing our experience to be as it is; it is possible to find each experience interesting no matter what is happening. External openness is a sense of adventure, enjoying the discovery of uncertainty, embracing the changes of impermanence.

Openness recognizes that each experience we have and every moment we are alive is a unique experience. When we are paying attention, we will notice these variations. The poet René Char said, "Each act is virgin, even the repeated ones." Yet the perceptual shortcuts that the brain takes can cut us off from experiencing the singularity of each moment (and the joy that comes from experiencing the uniqueness of this moment). The poet Stephen Dunn shared a similar sentiment: "Acknowledge that it takes long experience / in order to think of sameness / as an opportunity for imagination." Mindfulness meditation practice can be that long experience that makes it possible for us to open imagination.

Despite the wonderful opportunities afforded by openness, the mind is usually preoccupied with trying to seek comfort, often through foreclosing on the perception of now. The mind is often engaged in nothing other than an obsessive quest for reassurance, often through anticipating the future and reviewing the past. It's hard to be open with all that worry. When we can bring the mind to rest in the present moment, the energy that was going into rumination is now free to notice what is actually occurring. Without the pressure of needing to be comfortable *all* the time, we can enjoy this moment. We can be spacious.

- Openness starts with breathing in the here and now of this moment.
- Notice where your attention is right now and gently place it on the natural process of breathing. Let go of any expectations that may be boxing you in, or prejudicing you against simply resting your awareness in the moment.
- Let go of any storytelling about the past that may be weighing you down.

- When you can bring your attention to the specifics of this moment, receptivity will follow.
- Rest in a state of openness. Continue breathing for as long as you like. When you find expectations or rumination creeping in, gently release them and return your attention to the breath in the moment at hand.

Jettisoning any agenda opens you to surprise. You never know what might happen next and it doesn't matter. Your job in meditation is to attend to whatever is happening without judgment, control, or attempting to fix it. Let this next moment be an opportunity for inspiration.

Pain

One recent Fourth of July I ripped the tip of my finger open lifting a heavy stereo speaker that had very sharp points that secured it to the floor. I was rushing when I lifted one of the speakers; my mind was elsewhere. My initial response to this injury was angry self-recrimination. "You stupid *%#@*! idiot." The anger gave way to anxiety—visions of a crowded emergency department—after all, it was the Fourth of July and there were bound to be plenty of other mindless parties with recent tissue damage. Noticing the pain was not optional—it was an involuntary reaction. The other emotions were elective. My healthy response to this incident did not require anger and anxiety. My conditioned reactions were optional. I ran my finger under cold water, applied direct pressure, and then inspected the damage. I was certain I needed stitches, so I proceeded into town. Fortunately, the walk-in clinic was open and I didn't have to go to the main hospital ER. Shifting from "I can't believe this just happened" to "this has happened, now what?" eliminated the anguish I was feeling. Without the story, there was no pressure on me for things to be a particular way. I could accept things as they were in their perfect imperfection.

Pain is not a pleasant sensation, but it is sometimes necessary. The principal purpose of pain is to alert the brain to the presence of tissue damage or illness and to motivate appropriate action, as had been the case with my finger. Because of its value to our survival, pain is hardwired to rivet attention. These sensations are not easy to ignore, since they may contain crucial information.

This system works great when there is actionable information, but sometimes the signals from low level garden-variety aches and pains can also activate it, and our own minds can blow them out of proportion. On this basis we act like comfort-seeking missiles, as if our entire well-being depends on being comfortable and free from pain in every moment of our lives.

Every sensation of pain in the body has three elements—resistance (the sense of pressure that comes from contact of the body with the floor, furniture, clothes, and so forth), movement, and heat. We can "deconstruct" any bodily experience of pain into these elements and follow the patterns of physical resistance, movement, and heat. When we do this, the discomfort, irritation, or pain becomes impersonal. Our perceptions of pain become something like, "This is happening in such and such a way," versus "This is happening to me and I can't tolerate it." To apply this method in practice, try the following:

- When discomfort, an ache, or pain appears, begin to map it out—its contours, depth, breadth; anything you can notice about it. This will only take a few moments.
- Then investigate the three universal properties of resistance, movement, and heat. Aim for precision in your observations.
- You may notice pulsing, sharpness, or warmth. By paying close attention to these qualities of the pain, you will notice that the sensations are changing.
- What at first glance seemed solid is actually quite variable. Not only this, but when parsed into its constituent parts, pain becomes a dispassionate object of observation rather than something that we utterly identify with.
- Once personal narratives are divided from the sensation of pain, it tends to fade and is much more manageable.

An itch is an easy place to start. The reflexive impulse is to scratch each itch as it arises. We tend to do this automatically every time we have an itch, provided we can reach it. It is very common for itches to appear when we sit to meditate. One of the skills we must develop in order to make headway in our practice is the skill of not having our concentration derailed by every itch, ache, tickle, or discomfort. With practice, we come to understand that if we look closely into these sensations, they weaken and disperse, and the urgent need to fix them disappears.

Participation

There is a long tradition of socially and politically engaged Buddhism. As Thich Nhat Hanh said in his classic book *Peace Is Every Step,* "Mindfulness must be engaged. Once there is seeing, there must be acting. Otherwise, what is the sense of seeing?" Participation is predicated on the web of interconnectedness that defines life. Seeing this matrix of connectivity gives rise to wisdom: my actions are connected to everything else; if I act in selfish ways, others may be harmed. Participation stems from a sense of compassion that wishes to end suffering in the world, or at least to not contribute to it.

But participation alone is not enough. The attitude we strike as we participate is crucial. What is our motivation? Are we mindful as we engage? Are we feeling agitation, frustration, and anger toward the powers that be? If so, while what we do outwardly may be of some benefit, the distorted mindset that we harbor inwardly may actually contribute to the cycle of suffering. It's easy to get caught in this trap.

Another pitfall is prideful identification with being a compassionate person. This identity creates subtle tendrils of desire and aversion and, once again, the cycle of suffering is perpetuated. We look down at other people, easily frustrated and disappointed in their lack of compassion and other altruistic qualities. We end up wearing the garb of goodness outwardly, but inside we are still petty, negative, and reactive.

The sense that we are participating in the project of making this world what it is should become as natural to us as breathing. An awareness of whether or not we act rightly should accompany us every day as we move through the world. But we should be careful that our sense of participation doesn't become an empty act. It isn't enough to simply go through the steps of meeting the expectations others may have of people who are ethically engaged with the world around them. Our participation must be awake, fresh, and come naturally from the heart. A genuine sense of participation comes from carrying our practice off of the cushion into our lives.

We use the practice of mindfulness to work on ourselves first. By taming our own minds, we enact the basic principle of doing no harm. We must first become aware of how we treat ourselves. It can take quite a lot of energy to treat ourselves without violence, that is, without harsh, critical self-judgment. It can take quite a bit of practice to treat ourselves with forgiveness, empathy, and compassion. We establish a positive relationship to ourselves as a foundation for awakened action in the world. Armed with the knowledge that we are interconnected with all beings in the world, we can generalize the compassion we cultivate toward ourselves to others in the world.

Practicing in this way gives new meaning to the proverb "charity starts at home."

Path

There is an old Zen saying: "If you meet the Buddha on the road, kill him." The saying isn't meant to advocate killing actual buddhas, but it is a warning against preoccupation with the idealized state of buddhahood. If someone tells you he is enlightened, be cautious. If a guru says she is divine, be suspicious. Someone else's enlightenment won't magically enlighten you; you've go to do the work yourself. The old Zen masters knew the dangers of attachment to spiritual teachers. They knew that following even the Buddha blindly wouldn't get you far.

We are meant to walk the path that the Buddha discovered, tested, and taught, not worship it. We can test this path for ourselves. While the path has been worked out, seekers still have to navigate it for themselves. Like the running trail around my beloved Indian Brook Reservoir, the information that the path is there is useless unless I'm willing to make the effort to negotiate its twists and rises. We've got to actually walk the path to get anything out of it.

The Buddha's path is empirical: we can test it with our own experience. In fact, blind faith is an impediment to making progress on the path. Instead, we take the first step onto the Buddha's path by turning our attention to our own experience. The practice of mindfulness is one form that this turning of attention can take. Once we begin looking into the nature of our experience, we've actually taken our first tentative steps onto the path. The path can be secular or religious, formal or informal. You can work with a teacher or you can be self-directed. The path can take myriad forms.

The guidelines general to the path, whatever form it may take, are simple: don't harm yourself or others in deed, word, or thought; don't use your practice to bolster your ego; avoid preoccupation with material goods or status in relation to your practice; be genuine in your motives. It is useful to rely on an elder practitioner for guidance, but it is not an absolute requirement. Having comrades who share your practice is a great bolster to practice. It is always nice to have someone to talk to who understands the work you're attempting to do. The key to success in walking the path is to find, as Jack Kornfield says, "a path with heart"—that is, a path that you truly put your heart into.

But we must always be on guard against becoming attached to the path, against making the path into an ideal, somehow beyond our everyday experience. Such an idealization can actually become an obstacle. If my identity as a "Buddhist" or a "meditator" becomes just another source of self-centered behavior, then I have gone astray. The Buddha wasn't a Buddhist. He was simply a fellow human being seeking a way beyond suffering. He found his way to freedom, and did what he could to share his findings with others. We might think of him more as a spiritual physician than as a charismatic religious leader. His deepest hope was that others would use his own insights, like a patient taking medicine, to find a peace like that which he had found.

The truths that Buddha struggled with—suffering, old age, death, dissatisfaction—are as true today as they were in the ancient world. The medicinal path to recovery from these ills has been presented and preserved. The path awaits your steps.

Patience

Meditation brings up impatience in predictable fashion. We are just not used to sitting still for prolonged periods of time. Impatience presents a storyline about why the current situation is bad and why we need to change it immediately. Many times our Fear of Missing Out fans the flames of impatience. "There must be something better to do than this!"

When we notice this impatience theme, we can back away from the narrative and move into the body. The body will show us where impatience lives. By placing our attention there, we can investigate the nature of the restlessness that underlies the storyline. As with any emotion, impatience is comprised of energy that is changing in every moment.

Impatience is like an itch. It can feel overwhelming and pressing until it's gone only a few moments later. Can we leave it alone? Whenever you notice that impatience is present, pause and ask, "Where is this pressure coming from?" The question creates the opportunity to release that pressure. In most cases, you will realize that it is not necessary. It's just some idea that you need to be going faster. You can invite yourself to slow down. Pay attention to this moment. Impatience is a concept. Your life in this moment is not a concept, it's an *experience.*

Impatience is keyed to movement. When you feel impatient, you may become restless and want to move. When you sit in the crucible of meditation practice, you have the opportunity to cook impatience down to its elemental energy. As energy, it doesn't have any particular itinerary. You can hold it in stillness. Patience is curious about what is happening now, even if there doesn't seem to be much happening.

You can always pay attention to the simple and miraculous action of breathing. Patience knows that the quality of your experiences is more significant than the quantity of your experiences. Patience embodies confidence. "I am okay in this moment; I am happy to be where I am; and I don't need to add anything or take anything away."

Patience embodies wisdom. It's an economy of motion. When you embrace patience, you can sit still in your mind, not chasing every mental whim, impulse, and desire.

Perfectionism

Perfectionism can be a useful force when it serves the goal of quality, yet for most of us it seems to be a destructive force: impossible standards lead to procrastination instead of quality. The tyrannical pressure to achieve high standards becomes an obstacle in itself. There are the obvious forms of perfectionism and more subtle, insidious tendencies. We may feel a pressure in every moment for things to be a particular way and feel dissatisfied when they are not. Perfectionism is also about control and is, at its core, an attempt to cheat impermanence. We have the belief that if we can just get everything right, we won't be subject to the vicissitudes of life.

Perfectionism, when driven by an exaggerated measure for self-worth, is accountable to impossibly high self-imposed standards. We put undue, unreasonable, and unattainable pressure on ourselves. There is also a social component to perfectionism—managing the perceptions of others. The fear of judgment inhibits our work or just sucks the joy out of life. It is one thing to have high standards; it is another thing to peg our self-worth to the accomplishment of these standards.

I have a vivid memory from kindergarten. We were coloring mimeographed sheets with some design outlined by the purplish-blue lines that ancient reproduction technology produced. In my enthusiasm, I colored outside those lines. The meticulous girl sitting next to me colored within the lines. When she asked for another sheet to color in, she received it. When I asked for another opportunity, I was scolded for going outside the lines and denied. Miss Reed gave me an early lesson in contingent self-worth. If you don't do it perfectly, then you will not be rewarded. She implied there was something wrong with me for not conforming. If I don't color within the lines, then I am (fill in the blank): bad, lazy, defective, deficient, unworthy—and that day, left out. Zen master Shunryu Suzuki said, "Everything is perfect and there is always room for improvement." Short of a perfectomy, the Roshi's advice is a good starting point to liberate ourselves from perfectionism.

You can practice imperfection simply by sitting down to meditate. You will notice that your mind is anything but perfect. It gets distracted, absorbed in petty stories, and doesn't want to sit still. You can practice coloring outside the lines in other areas of your life. Whenever you notice the anxiety that arises when you haven't met some imposed standard, you can sit with it, locate it in the body, and breathe into it. You are perfect in your imperfection. Embracing your imperfection is not an invitation to avoid making goals; it is an encouragement not to be attached to these aims and their outcomes to the extent that it gets in the way with your progress. A healthier relationship to the actions of our lives is found in focusing on the action at hand. When you are attached, you are at risk for the stridency, recrimination, and judgments that make perfectionism stressful. A healthier relationship to the actions of our lives is found in focusing on the process not the outcome.

You can start to let go the moment you label something as perfectionistic. You can inquire into its necessity. You can authorize yourself to be as you are—imperfect. You can work hard without beating yourself up. You are bound to get more done and have better results when you put less pressure on yourself. An open hand can accomplish more than a closed hand. While a fist may have the ability to punch through something, that is about all it can do. An open hand can be firm; it can guide, manipulate (in a good way), and can keep us moving in a beneficial direction. The alternative to the fist of perfectionism is the open hand of acceptance.

Permission

I arrived at IMS—the Insight Meditation Society—for a ten-day retreat. It was summer 1992, I had finished my course work, and my dissertation was underway. It was a fine time to devote myself to intensive practice. Yet I found myself restless, edgy, and unsettled. While I had scheduled myself to be at this retreat, I hadn't given myself permission to be there—to show up and give myself fully to the practice. Resistance was beneath the surface of my busy mind and only revealed itself in the quiet of the retreat. "What are you doing here?" "You should be working on your dissertation." "What's the point of meditation anyway?"

Mindfulness practice invites us to give ourselves permission to be however we are. This granting of permission is a way to think about the practice. We are so conditioned to action that if we are not constantly doing something "productive" then we feel like something is wrong. Just sitting and breathing seems downright un-American. When I teach meditation now, I provide the instructions: "Give yourself permission to do nothing other than pay attention to your breathing."

Imagine being stranded in a place where there is no phone, nothing to read, no one to talk to, and nothing to write on. No Twitter. No Facebook. Think of the unpossibilities! It would be normal to have an initial flush of anxiety being unplugged from all these sources of input. After we finish freaking out, we just might settle into what is happening now. Paying attention to the moment-by-moment arising and disappearing of experiences can be fascinating. A mindfulness meditation retreat is akin to this stranded scenario. Noble silence is a process of setting aside all of our usual distractions with a commitment to explore our experience just as it is for an extended period of time. This could be an afternoon, a day, a week, ten days, three months, or even longer.

A retreat requires deep permission. We must extricate ourselves from our work schedule and set aside all of our responsibilities. We must grapple with the fear that somehow the world needs us at the helm of busyness in order to keep functioning. We must wrestle with the even bigger concern that we'll go away and things will move along fine without us.

If we want to get to the quietest reaches of the mind, I don't know any other way to get there other than the retreat environment. Once we settle into being there—once the permission has been granted—a wonderful discovery can take place. Hour after hour we are with the process of being—breathing, sitting, walking, eating. The stories that comprise our selves may eventually fall away. Bliss may fill the gap left by the departure of "I, me, and mine." When there is no "self" to catalogue suffering, there can be no sense of deprivation, since there is nothing to deprive. We move from one experience to another and, if there is no scorekeeper, suffering flows like water through our fingers.

Start with giving yourself permission to be in this moment. You are breathing. You are reading. You are sitting. Authorize your attention to be with *this* moment, relinquishing what has elapsed and not reaching out for what has yet to come. You can grant your consent to any moment you are living. Practice this throughout the rest of your day. Whatever you are doing—give yourself permission to do it without caveat, restraint, or regret.

Play

My dogs Harley and Sumi know how to play, and they spend hours doing so. When they met for the first time, they lapsed into a spontaneous romp through a snow-packed Smuggler's Notch. They ran at full speed, biting and wrestling, changing directions, rearing like bucks and falling down. They took turns being dominant. They haven't stopped playing since. They play inside too, nuzzling, necking, and clacking their teeth together. They are exuberance, energy, and affection.

We adult humans and our work-ethic driven culture could learn something from dogs. Researcher Stuart Brown has shown that play is anything but frivolous and not just for kids. Play is part of our genetic inheritance and serves important developmental biological and survival functions. As infants, contact with primary caretakers (still mostly moms) sets the stage for play. Play starts with the developmental process of attunement, critical for healthy brain development. Attunement is mother's skill in paying attention and responding to the subtle and obvious needs of her infant. Play is the base for attunement. Play is a way of interfacing with the world without purpose other than exploring, having fun, and seeking pleasure. It can involve jumping, manipulating objects, rough and tumble movements, social play, spectating, imagination, and storytelling (all of these are developing skills for the child). Even meditation can be play. Brown notes, "Play is born by curiosity and exploration."

It's too bad that as a culture we don't nurture play into adulthood. I view play as vital to *exquisite self-care* and something that we should do often and with others. Play often provides a spontaneous form of mindfulness. We naturally fall into mindfulness when we are engaged in play. Having fun holds great power to move us into the present moment. Fun isn't frivolous; play is necessary for health.

Mindfulness practice can be a form of play when we drop into this moment with a sense of exploration, endeavoring to see what is present. We touch what arises playfully—neither trying to own it nor get rid of it. When we can be here with what is happening, the energy that was going into trying to fix things can now go into enjoying things. When you find yourself feeling tense, stressed, or harried, pause and take a few mindful breaths. Having grounded yourself in the present moment of your body, you can now look for an opportunity to transform being ill-at-ease into something more playful.

One way to effect this coup is to engage your full attention with the task at hand. This requires cessation of resistance and a relinquishing of complaint. You can become pure activity and that will feel more like play. A few minutes of mindfulness can always be helpful, whether sitting, walking, or standing. Perhaps a few yoga postures or doing something silly like standing on your head in public (if you have that yoga move in your repertoire). If you are at work, you may need to be subtler about your play break, but you could try skipping down the corridor. Smiling, laughing, or singing might just do the trick too. If you have dogs, get down on the floor and play with them. They'll always be game to do so. If you are at home, one easy form of play is dancing around your living room to your favorite music. I do it all the time.

Procrastination

A lot of my patients come to me for help with procrastination. It's a particularly knotty issue and one with deep, layered causes. It goes right down to our core beliefs around self, the habits we've established over a lifetime, and messages we've imported from the culture. I've written all of the entries for this book through to Z, except one; I've left "procrastination" for last. I've been procrastinating on procrastination!

Our very identity is bound up in what we do. We live within the message that *doing* must be purposeful, productive, and perfect. The stakes are high. Under those circumstances, it's not hard to imagine that anxiety might accompany our attempts to act in the world. Fear of consequences—dreaded "what ifs"—bring anxiety. "What if it's a waste of time?" "What if I fail?" "What if I make a fool of myself?" "What if it's not perfect?"

Forgive me for spoiling the suspense—whatever it is that we do, it will not be perfect. All of these "what ifs" can conspire to inaction— procrastination. If we don't act, then we don't have to confront the feared outcomes. In this way, procrastination becomes a specialized case of aversion—the tendency to avoid things that are unpleasant.

In this culture, we are not comfortable with simply *being*—the raw sense of aliveness can be scary. We often procrastinate on creative tasks that can bring us precariously close to the edge of rawness—that sense of not knowing what will issue forth next—the words written on the page, the colors on the canvas, the movement and emotions that arise from losing ourselves in the music. We may not know what to do with the grandeur of being alive in this moment. We may try to control it and in the process of doing so squeeze out of spontaneity, losing our freedom to act.

Mindfulness can help with procrastination. As with any feeling, you can explore procrastination in your body. First, find its location. Next, map out how it feels. You can notice the sensations of physical resistance, movement, and temperature. You can bring your attention back from the storylines of procrastination to its energy as it unfolds moment-by-moment. You can recite the intention to relinquish perfectionism to move forward with the action that is stuck. Aim for "good enough." Shoot for 80 percent. You may wind up getting more. By investigating procrastination with mindful attention, you can begin to notice how it inhabits your mind. Procrastination, as with any concept, becomes more pliable when you can name it, explore it in the body, and familiarize yourself with the thoughts that promote it. After you touch it with mindfulness, you create a space where you can make a choice. One option is to keep procrastinating. Another option is to move forward with imperfect action, allowing that to be sufficient to move to the next moment and the moment after that.

Quality

Riding on a motorcycle is dangerous. Actually, driving a car is nearly as dangerous; we are just cut off from this fact because we are ensconced in steel and glass. On the motorcycle, the quality of our attention matters. Setting aside fear is a prerequisite to that quality. If our attention wavers, injury or death may not be far behind. It is like meditating with your hair on fire—with a sense of urgency to pay attention no matter what, as if our lives depended upon it.

Quality is taking this moment seriously, seeking the fresh, direct experience of now. Quality is this moment and nothing else. Quality recognizes that life is fragile, precious, and unpredictable. When the road races by my feet a few inches away at 80 mph, I know quality. Motorcycle riding is an exceptional way to bring mindfulness into life. I also seek the same quality riding the slopes of my Northern Vermont landscape on a snowboard. The consequences of attention lapses sliding down a frozen mountain at 50 mph are not quite as acute as highway speeds on a motorcycle, but still formidable.

Quality is showing up for the moment, giving it everything that we have to give, not holding back. Storyteller John Schraven tells a parable about a carpenter. This carpenter worked many years producing high quality custom homes. One day he realized he had done enough—he was exhausted, burned out. He decided to retire. His employer implored him to build one more home. The carpenter did so, but grudgingly. He gave it a half-hearted effort, using poor quality materials, cutting corners, and just walking through the job. He chose not to follow his previous impeccable path of quality. When he finished the job, his employer handed him a set of keys. "This house is yours. It is my gift to you for your years of service." Quality never takes a vacation. We "phone it in" at our peril.

Mindfulness is CQI—continuous quality improvement. When we practice, we refine our mind's ability to know itself. When we practice, we hone our mind's ability to engage with this moment as if it really mattered. Mindfulness practice helps us to know where we are in any given moment. When we are in contact with the moment, we can stay with the moment. When we have departed from the quality of now into fantasy and memory, we become skilled at redirecting our attention to what matters most now.

The more skilled we become at mindfulness, the more we notice how our moments are lacking in quality. This is a seeming paradox of mindfulness. The more we notice, the more we notice that we are not noticing. Once we notice, quality can follow in the next moment. R. D. Laing says, "The range of what we think and do is limited by what we fail to notice. And because we fail to notice there is little we can do to change until we notice how failing to notice shapes our thoughts and deeds."

We can build our own homes of experience in every moment. If we don't pay attention, cut corners, and sleepwalk through these moments, we will miss the special quality of life that is available now. Mindfulness brings quality to this and every moment.

Quiet

The world is noisy. Our twenty-four-hour society has made the experience of quietude elusive. The presence of "smart" technology has made the problem worse. We are always on, always available. We run the risk of becoming infomaniacs, constantly checking for tweets, texts, emails, and status updates. In today's world, we need to seek quiet in a deliberate way. Meditation provides this opportunity for quiet. On one hand, we are desperate for quiet; on the other hand, we may be ill-equipped to tolerate it.

Mindfulness helps to rehabilitate us back into quiet. Formal practice requires that we step out of our usual routines to sit still on a cushion for some period of time each day. Part of what makes mindfulness such a powerful healing technology are these relatively silent gaps in the otherwise constant flux of bustling activity. We need time just to be, and mindfulness practice fulfills this need.

While practicing, we develop our inner quietude. Like all the busyness of our days, the mind is busy too, constantly talking to itself about this, that, and the other. The mind, likewise, needs respite from this constant activity. Brain researchers have demonstrated that mindfulness meditation takes us out of what is known as the default mode network of brain functioning. This network is narrative and self-referential and noticed as the constant onslaught of thoughts, images, and emotions. Mindfulness practice develops the skill to extricate ourselves from the default mode network at will. This capacity is correlated with a number of benefits that include decreased stress and increased empathy.

I think we are uncomfortable with silence, hence the "awkward silence" in conversations. There is an implied pressure to fill up those moments with something—even idle chatter will do. Why not try this experiment:

- Just sit and be with another person without talking.
- Notice the urge to fill in the silence with nonverbal communications—nodding, smiling, and so forth. Let go of even nonverbal communication, taking quiet even into the mind.
- Try just being.
- Add nothing.
- Relax and breathe, just being.

Having done this exercise with many groups, I can predict that this may be difficult for you. It will take some getting used to. Interpersonal quiet can be an alien landscape.

When we invite quiet into our lives through silence of activity, technology, communication, and mind, new possibilities may present themselves. With practice, quiet can become a faithful friend—and an informative friend, too. There are other things going on in the world when we take the time to be still. These gifts await us when we invite stillness from within and without.

Reality

I am running on a mountain trail, but instead of paying attention to the terrain I am encased in my imagination. I'm rehearsing a conversation that I might have later, anticipating that it won't go well: that it will be tense, contentious, adversarial. I feel the conviction that I am *right* in this fantasy scenario. Suddenly, I am on the ground having just tripped over a root jutting up from the trail. Reality has asserted itself and knocked me out of fantasy. We can live large patches of our lives lost in fictions like the one I had while trail running. Mindfulness gives us the option of attending to the real and not just accidentally stumbling upon it when reality asserts itself. We can seek out reality in every moment—we can touch it with our senses as we move through the world. Every moment presents the choice between reverie and reality. Left to habit, we'll fall into the imaginary and maybe fall to the ground too.

If you read about Eastern philosophy, even Buddhism, you may come across descriptions of *ultimate reality*, whatever that is. The question of ultimate reality has been vexing philosophers, theologians, and scientists for millennia. The Buddha threw his hat in the ring. The difference between his philosophy and many others is that it was not speculative—it came from his direct experience. For the Buddha, all that mattered was the ground is hard and it hurts when you fall down on it. The metaphysics of ultimate nature is a distraction from the practical lived experience. This insistence on the practical makes his insights more of an introspective psychology than a metaphysical religion and a stark contrast to the belief systems of his time—for example, Brahmanism, that saw human experience as an inferior version of some ultimate reality.

The goal of Brahmanic spiritual practice was to transcend the mundane to rejoin Brahma—the definitive reality lying beyond the world of appearances. The Buddha rejected this notion. The deep insights the Buddha had during his meditation revealed something different. He saw that reality is constructed through an interaction of our senses, including mind, and the world "out there." We can only come to know the constituent processes of perception, feeling, and consciousness, not some reality independent of these. In other words, the ground doesn't hurt until I hit it—it doesn't have an essential "hurtfulness." The self is no different than the ground. The Buddha rejected the idea of an immortal soul because he saw how our experience is assembled moment-by-moment through the flux of different processes between so-called "mind" and "matter." In other words, there is no foundation, heart, or core—nothing ultimate. *Everything* comes into being in mutual dependence—they coarise, moment-by-moment. It's all phenomena; there's no numina (vital spirit or guiding force). Again, this was a *radical* view for his time. It is a view that has *radical* implications for today. There is nothing, including "me," that comes into being independent of this constant flux. "I" didn't hit the ground. Of course, one could see my body falling to the ground. However, the subjective experience of "me" was woven into the fabric of falling. I didn't fall. I *was* falling. Who I was and how I was emerged from the particular constellation of factors occurring in that moment.

If there is no "there" there, then there is only here! We are not somehow standing outside of this flux observing—we are that flux; we are inextricably that fluidity and nothing more. This recognition opens the way for the self to become a process that is free rather than a thing that can suffer (i.e., no-*thing*, no suffering). If reality is phenomenological (focusing on the process of here and now) rather than ontological (trying to figure out ultimate things) then we can be okay no matter what the conditions are in this moment. If reality is all process, then there is no absolute reference standard. There are no things to configure, no things to protect. The Buddha observed we have the capacity to be happy when we give ourselves the opportunity to do so—when we don't *thing* ourselves into anguish. We have profound capacities for well-being that await this philosophical shift from thing-ness to process-ness.

When I am the process, I am enjoying my movement along the path, the sun, the rain, the clouds, the birds, and the presence of the rocky woods. When I'm lost in my fantasy conversations, I've left the process and have reverted to being a thing—"me"—that needs protecting from imaginary insults among other things. When I catch myself lost in self-referencing conversations or when reality has to remind me by knocking me to the ground, I can resume the process of enjoying the woods. Without meditation practice, however, it may be difficult to take advantage of this shift.

Meditation is a process that can help us to deconstruct these mistaken ideas—experientially. When you practice mindfulness you shift back and forth between fantasy and reality. Reality is the feeling of your breath precisely now; fantasy is wondering what's for lunch: "How much longer until meditation is over?" Fantasy is the complaint about your stiff back. Reality is the sensations that give rise to the plaintive missive. Those sensations have a location, a sense of spread, pressure, and temperature. Reality is the experience of being alive now; fantasy is the concept of "me" having this life. When you meditate, you endeavor to come back to reality over and over again.

Regret

The contemporary, Buddhist-influenced bard Eddie Vedder of the band Pearl Jam sings in his song "Present Tense" from the album *No Code*:

You can spend your time alone redigesting past regrets,
or you can come to terms and realize
that you're the only one who can't forgive yourself.
It makes much more sense to live in the present tense.

Regret is normal and adaptive. When we can learn something from a situation wherein we've erred, it makes us better people. But many times regret becomes an end in itself. Instead of providing feedback, regret becomes an obsession. We scrutinize everything we've done with critical judgment, looking to build a case against ourselves. Regret, when handled improperly, can become strictly the province of the "contingent self" that bases its worth on what other people think (or at least what we imagine other people think) or on our failure to live up to self-imposed standards.

Regret eats up energy that could be applied to making this moment more productive. Retrospection has a purpose when it supports the development of wisdom. If the aim of looking backward is self-castigation, this looking backward is its own unskillful action. Not only were we damaged by the original unskillful action, we are compounding that damage through the violence of self-judgment. Unproductive regret interferes with our ability to skillfully respond to the demands of this moment.

Mindfulness can examine regret, feel its hot flush in the body, and follow its sensations rather than its storyline. When attention wanders during meditation, you may find regret arising, and when you catch yourself, a choice emerges. If you berate yourself, the present moment remains elusive. The difference between the expert and the novice is not the absence of mind-wandering; the difference is what each does when those departures occur. The expert moves on to the next moment, whereas the novice is more likely to fixate on the lapse in attention—complaining, fussing, regretting. With much practice, we learn not to associate our identity as meditators so closely with the steadfastness of our concentration. Concentration is impermanent, just like everything else. But when we are newcomers to the practice, how well we concentrate feels integral to our own sense of self-worth as meditators. Before we get this habit in check, meditation may become a source of unproductive regret.

- When your attention begins to ruminate on regrets—reviewing past events, as if by doing so the damage could be undone—remind yourself that this event has passed and is no longer happening, and practice the gentle return to the breath in the moment.
- Even if the immediate aftereffects of a regretted act are still felt, remind yourself that the act has passed and is no longer present, and give yourself permission to let go of regret.
- Rather than ruminate on regret, practice saying "Thank you" to your regrets. Treat them as teachers that show you what not to do again in the future. Thank regret, and practice gently returning your attention to the breath in the moment.

We can learn from our mistakes when we make them. When we learn that, in retrospect, something we have done was unskillful, we can learn from our lack of skill. When approached from the right perspective, we can be grateful for anything that happens. Skillful actions bring their own rewards, and unskillful actions can be opportunities to learn.

Relationships

I learned a lot from my failed marriage: humility, the location of my blind spots, where I needed to deepen my mindfulness practice, where I was vulnerable, and what my untapped strengths were. All relationships are teachers, especially the difficult ones.

We might think of enlightenment as something that one does alone, in solitude. We don't typically think of enlightenment as happening for someone who has a mate and is juggling kids, a career, and a household. But contemporary spiritual practice more often than not happens in situations like this. Relationships with others—our spouses, lovers, parents, children, siblings, bosses, coworkers, friends, and pets—pervade our lives. Relationships ought not to be thought of as obstacles on the spiritual path. In many ways, relationships are the very stuff of spiritual practice. In many ways, practice is easier if one is celibate in a monastery, rather than committed to someone out in the bustle of society. Being able to put our spiritual training to work is essential for laypeople.

Mindfulness teacher Diana Winston makes the case that mindfulness practice is nothing other than the practice of love. It becomes love by training us to say yes to our lives. "Because as you sit there, hour after hour, you learn to say yes. Yes to your jagged breathing, yes to your itchy scalp. Yes to the leaf blower dude across the street, yes to your grief and pain and shame and grandiosity and fear. Not because you want to act on these things, but because they're true, and fleeting, and simply part of who you are." If we can say yes to the conditions of our lives, we can open to the conditions of being with another because sharing a space always brings less than ideal conditions.

Being in a relationship is a potent teacher because others function like a mirror showing us where we cling and where we push away. Being with others helps us to discover implicit rules we follow, secondary agendas we may harbor, and unhealthy attachments we may not be aware that we have. Despite the value of solitude, if we never intimately interact with others, we might never learn these important things about ourselves. Intimate relationships, in particular, require vulnerability and give us the opportunity to uncover our own patterns of reactivity and the defensiveness that protects us from really acknowledging our own shortcomings. In our vulnerability we allow our imperfections to show, and because we care about our partners, we are willing to be open to feedback.

A relationship can be the crucible that tests the mettle of our mindfulness. When you maintain a levelheaded perspective on others, even when they may be testing your limits or pushing your buttons, it is a sign of deepening mindfulness. Each moment in the life of a relationship can be a teacher.

- When you notice distress arising in response to something a friend or loved one has said or done, pause and ask yourself, "What can I awaken to here?"
- Remember that the same basic humanity, the desire to find happiness and avoid suffering, motivates your partner in a relationship, too. Be patient with harsh words or anger.
- Your own feelings may reveal deeply conditioned personal beliefs about how things should be. Be open to examining such beliefs and ask yourself if they are worth preserving.
- Speak your own truth, share what you feel, but do so in a way that is compassionate and considerate.

Restraining reactivity and speaking truth requires courage and the willingness to approach disagreement differently. When you can set aside the need to be right, a world of possibility opens up. Changing your perspective on relationships can lead to insight and insight can lead to wisdom.

Resilience

My therapist once reminded me of a bike race that I had done—the Whiteface Challenge. This race took place on the winding toll road that ascends Whiteface Mountain in the Adirondacks. It is eight miles long with an 8 percent average grade. That's long and steep. At the time, I was training for a triathlon, so I decided to ride my heavy mountain bike with a twenty-pound pack on my back to make it even more of a challenge. There were only a handful of mountain bikers among the hundreds of entrants. Everyone else was on a road bike. I couldn't comprehend this at first but soon learned why—the ascent was unrelenting and seemingly interminable. I persisted, one cadence after another, until I reached the summit. From there I could enjoy the magnificent views and then the thrilling ride back down. I used my memory of ascending Whiteface to hold me through the divorce process. The ascent was a metaphor. It required tenacity in the moment, stamina, and there would be a resolution if I kept moving my legs, one push after another. That image helped me to maintain a modicum of equanimity and to keep up with the work of life.

Resilience is the ability to bounce back from adversity and a flexibility that lessens the impact of adversity. Resilience is persistence. Resilience is a key benefit of mindfulness. Being mindful will not prevent all distress from arising, but when it does arise, the skill of mindfulness will help us to recognize it, disengage from it, and return to baseline more rapidly. Without mindfulness, there is a tendency to stay stuck in a difficult moment. If rumination is our habit, mindfulness can help us keep from digging deeper into the situation.

Resilience seeks to highlight then abandon what I call the "secondary agenda." In any situation, there is a primary agenda—whatever it is that we are doing now. However, it is rare that the primary agenda is the only agenda. We usually add to it expectations, conditions, needs, contingencies. It is as if, in order for us to be okay, things have to turn out a certain way. The poem "The Jeweler" by the Sufi ecstatic Hafiz, from the collection *I Heard God Laughing: Poems of Hope and Joy,* captures this sense of abandoning the secondary agenda.

> But one moment with me, my dear,
> Will show you
> That there is nothing,
> Nothing
> Hafiz wants from you.

When we give ourselves to this moment, wholeheartedly, there is nothing to want. When we focus on the process rather than the outcome, joy comes along for the ride.

Resilience is the key to adapting to the world. It allows us to bend without breaking, to recover from the inevitable challenges of daily life, and to engage with confidence rather than the dictates of secondary agendas.

Resistance

I ate too much at dinner and while meditating and I had a bellyache. Quite mild, mind you, but enough to give rise to distress. I was pushing against the discomfort, not wanting it to be present—yet it was present. What was the point of pushing?

Pointless resistance is what Buddhists would call "delusion." My view of things was misguided, mistaken, muddled. I was wishing for something that could not exist in this moment and by futilely pursuing it I was causing myself more discomfort. The state of my belly was the state of my belly. It was an experience. I could sit with the sensations or resist them. That was my choice. Resistance in cases like this is not only ineffective at providing relief, but it takes energy.

There is no wisdom in this kind of resistance. My energy would have been better spent contemplating the greed that overshadowed my actions at dinner that evening than trying to fix my full belly after the fact. I experienced the karmic consequences of my choices. I ate too much; my stomach hurt: cause and effect.

When we resist, we become like a solid object. Picture a structure with louvered panels, much like a window blind, that stands in the wind. When the louvers are closed, they provide ample surface for the wind to push against. If the wind blows hard enough, it will knock the structure down. Now imagine these louvers open with only their edges set against the wind. Now their threshold to the wind is almost imperceptible—a thin slice that offers little resistance to the wind's force. The wind that knocks down a *resisting* structure cannot topple an *accepting* one. When we practice mindfulness, we mustn't give whatever experiences appear to our minds anything to push against.

When we are in the moment, it's as if we've opened the louvers of our mind so as not to resist the wind of experience. Without resistance we are more resilient and more able to withstand whatever comes at us.

- Resistance appears as an inclination that says, "I don't want this."
- When you recognize resistance creeping into your attitude, name it for what it is—just an impulse, an inclination, a thought. If you can name it, you can tame it.
- Sometimes resistance appears as an energy in the body. When we are mentally resistant, often our physical body will grow more rigid as well. Be on the lookout for signs of tension in the body. When noted, relax the body and the mind, return the attention to the breath.
- As is the case with most mindsets that can interfere with meditation, learning to recognize and disarm resistance is key.

One cold winter evening after work, I got into my car bracing against the single digit temperature. I was not happy about the situation. I was shivering. I noticed that I was also tensing up against the cold, as if that could somehow hold it off. Reminding myself that "cold Buddha shivers," I relaxed my body and felt the cold for what it was, just a sensation. Once I let go of resistance, the cold was just cold and the misery of it vanished.

Restlessness

Energy arises from the bottoms of my feet, ascends my legs, tingling its way up to my torso, and by the time it reaches my fingers that ought to be typing on the keyboard, I am out of my chair and pacing around the house. Without constant vigilance, restlessness pushes me around— gets me out of my seat and away from the task at hand. My mind does

not want to sit still reading, writing, or editing. It wants to be doing
something—anything—else.

If you have done any meditating, you know all about restlessness. As
a beginner, restlessness may set in even just a few minutes after you've
sat down, once the novelty of the concept of meditating has worn off.
But even longtime meditators get restless if they sit long enough. The
body and mind can become uncomfortable, edgy, and uneasy. Naturally, we'll want relief when that happens. But one part of developing a
good practice is being able to get a handle on restlessness. Here are a
few techniques that might help you to do this:

- Fidgeting happens when autopilot has already taken over.
  When you find yourself fidgeting, pause, note that it has
  happened, and return your attention to the breath.
- Be mindful of the body. Notice when restless energy begins
  to build, and you begin to feel that you want to move or shift
  your position on the cushion.
- Many times a narrative of discomfort feeds the desire to
  move. Ask yourself, "Where does my mind think it needs to
  go in order to be okay?"
- Many times, when we fall into habitual stories—about so-
  and-so who's such a jerk, or about recurring problems at
  work, for example—our bodies respond to these thoughts:
  tension may build in the shoulders and neck, we may be
  unconsciously clenching our jaws, or our leg muscles may
  begin to tense up. Noting the relationship between certain types of stories we get involved in during practice and
  restlessness in the body will help us to recognize potential
  causes of restlessness much earlier.
- If restlessness comes in the form of wanting to respond to an
  itch or a tickle, try approaching the sensation with a sense
  of interest. Examine the itch, letting your attention enter
  it, turn it over, and pick it apart. In many cases examining
  sensations in the body causes them to disperse.

Early on in my life as a meditator, I attended a ten-day retreat led by S. N. Goenka. By day six I was plotting my escape! I was sure that I had reached my limit; I couldn't sit still for one more minute. Luckily, that evening Goenka shared with us the story of his first retreat. He surprised me by saying that he too had been planning his escape over the walls of the compound. But, with encouragement, he let go of the fantasy of escape and stuck with the practice for the remainder of the retreat. His own story encouraged me to work with my restlessness. By resting my mind on the disquieting energy in my body, rather than weaving that energy into a story of how awful it felt, I found peace in the midst of what seemed like internal chaos.

The answer to restlessness is not set ourselves in motion, but to remain at rest with awareness.

Revolution

A mindfulness revolution is happening in the West, driven in large part by therapeutic applications of mindfulness. A proliferation of mindfulness-based therapies and an explosion of research have fueled this development. Of the hundreds of research studies that have been conducted on mindfulness-based interventions, over 75 percent have been published in the past five years. This percentage continues to increase as more and more studies are conducted.

Most major medical centers in the United States have some mindfulness training programs, and MBSR (Mindfulness Based Stress Reduction) programs can be found all around the globe. Mick Krasner and Ronald Epstein at the University of Rochester Medical School train physicians, residents, and medical students to be more empathetic and less burned-out. At Georgetown Medical School, Adi Haramati teaches students mindfulness practice along with other mind-body disciplines. My small contribution to the mindfulness revolution is my daily practice. I also teach, conduct workshops, write books, and blog about mindfulness. I am one of the many voices in a growing chorus.

In one sense the mindfulness revolution is like a political revolution—we martial our minds to overthrow ignorance. Our work is to rouse ourselves from the state of automatic pilot, to cast off the chains of storytelling, and to meet the world with open eyes, as it is. A feeling of dissatisfaction with our lives motivates many of us: "Why do I always fall into negative ways of thinking and acting? Why is it so hard to change? Why am I so stressed all of the time?" Once the fire to take hold of ourselves and begin to consciously direct the flow of our lives is lit, we take to the cushion like protesters taking to the street. And of course the changes we work toward reach much farther than the cushion, into our everyday lives and interactions with others.

In another sense, mindfulness is like a revolution in the sense of coming full circle. The very heart of our practice is to come back to now. When our minds wheel out into fantasy and storytelling, we bring it back to the breath, to the moment at hand. As we carry our practice into the busyness of our daily lives, we slip into self-judgment, storytelling, and worry, and bring ourselves back, over and over again. We make these revolutions countless times per day. These revolutions may not be predictable, like the earth revolving around the sun, but they occur nonetheless.

So each time you sit down to your practice, you are taking part in the revolution against distraction, confusion, and ignorance. You are also taking part in the revolution of the mind back to the breath, back to the moment at hand. The revolution moves on as the breath revolves in and out of the body. When we follow that cycle with attention, we water the seeds of insight and eventual awakening. Each time we reclaim attention back from the future, past, or commentary, we tend the delicate shoots of change.

Like any revolution, there may be fits and starts. Mindfulness may be front and center in full effect one day and lagging the next. Persistence is the key to effecting change. Each instance of retrieving our attention from the future, past, or commentary is a minirevolution against the powerful forces of habit.

¡Viva la revolución!

Sangha

At the weekly meditations that I used to host at the Exquisite Mind Studio, we'd sit in a rectangular "circle" around the perimeter of the room. One day the energy in the room felt particularly strong. One of the participants likened us to a mushroom circle, as she felt the energy moving around our ring. She described the feeling inside of her as Perrier bubbles.

Mushrooms connect to each other in underground networks forming a collective organism. The *sangha* is the community of people who follow the teachings of the Buddha, or more generically, anyone who engages in mindfulness meditation. When the sangha meets, we touch that invisible, underground sense of connectedness that gets obscured by the busyness and the stories of "me" that otherwise engulf us.

On that Thursday afternoon, the energy that enveloped us perhaps came from that subterranean connectedness. In the "middle world" of Newtonian physics, we don't appreciate the interconnectedness of everything. Boundaries appear to be distinct. Walls are walls. The laws of physics apply in exacting ways. We appear to be separate entities. But there is more to the world than what we see. We can only see what our sensory organs and brain processing allow us to see, but there is more going on here. At some level, we are all one energy with no clear boundaries. Perhaps we get a glimpse of that when we meditate. Whether we actually connect, it certainly feels as if we do.

The Buddha turned people on to the dharma and his early followers formed the original sangha. Followers of the Buddha then, as now, seek to validate the truth of his teaching in their own experience. So we are not following the Buddha's wisdom based on faith. The sangha is not a religion; it was, and is, a collective of seekers meditating to realize a truth about life and the possibility of awakening. The sangha is one of the oldest continuous human institutions, albeit an informal one. There is no central hierarchy. The group meeting in your town is part of the sangha just as was the group meeting in the Jetavana grove 2,500 years ago. The intention is the same—meditate with an eye toward liberation.

The Buddha eschewed central organization. He did not name a successor. He felt the dharma should be the guide, not a person. Formal lineages have developed, especially in the Zen and Tibetan traditions, but this was long after the time of the Buddha.

The Buddha cited the sangha as one of the Triple Jewels along with the dharma and what the Buddha represented—the possibility of awakening. These three are sufficient for the path to awakening. The Buddha, again, is not the figurehead of the historical Buddha but buddha—the capacity for transformation that we all have. Dharma is the Buddha's collected teachings and more importantly the truth that these teachings point to. Sangha brings buddha and dharma together—binds, connects, and inspires the efforts of practice. The sangha works. It not only feels good to practice together, but communal sitting supports the practice. When our minds wander, the presence of others in the room will help to remind us to come back. We will sit up straighter and engage with more effort. The opportunity to practice together is a precious opportunity. Find a sangha where you are. If there isn't a group sitting nearby, you can invite your friends over to meditate. Online communities are also forming, like the one supported by *Tricycle* magazine (check it out at tricyle.org).

Kalyanamitra (Sanskrit) or *kalyanamitta* (Pali) refers to the "spiritual friend." This friend can be a spiritual teacher that guides on the path but also refers to peers that travel the path along with you. The sangha would then be comprised of spiritual friends, supporting each other in the work to awaken.

Sangha is a commitment to practice and to supporting the practice of others. If you are a strong sitter and can practice on your own, consider sharing that strength with people who founder in solitude. If you struggle when you practice alone, seek out a community where others can support you. We are all in this together—all struggling to bring a modicum of awakening into life in all its imperfections. Together, we can be a mushroom circle—rooted underground—to form connections that sustain us.

Self

Who are you? Emily Dickinson would reply:

> I'm nobody! Who are you?
> Are you nobody, too?

Most of us would naturally reply, "I am me." More precisely, though, I am *a* me, one of many who have a sense of self. The Buddha's most radical idea was there actually is no self that corresponds to this sense—at least not in the unexamined way we typically experience it. Of course, there is someone here to be called "me" who lives at a certain address and has been alive for however long I've been alive. But this is just a matter of conventions. When I examine this "me," really dig into what it is and where it's located, it is quite difficult to pin down.

Am I my body? Am I my mind? If I try to pin my self to the body, I find that the body itself is made of many things, each of which seems to have its own identity as well. I may look at my hand and say "That's me," but if I lose that hand in an accident, the "me" still remains, now just a handless me. It's even more difficult to pin the self to the mind.

The mind is like the wind: formless, insubstantial, moving wherever it likes unimpeded. Is my self my thoughts? If so, which ones? It would seem odd for my enduring self to be as fleeting as are my thoughts. Is my "self" love, or hate, or indifference? Am I my memories, or dreams, or imagination? When I examine the body and mind that I refer to as my self, I am confronted with myriad constituents, each reducible into constituents of its own, none of which seem to be candidates worthy of the name "me."

Another problem I am faced with is the seeming regularity of my self. I have felt that I am "me" as long as I can remember. This sense of being "me" at the heart of identity seems to remain the same from day to day, year to year, and decade to decade. But how can this be? I cannot possibly be the same "me" as I was when a baby. This is unthinkable either physically or mentally. There isn't an atom of my body that existed at that time, and I can certainly say that my present mind is definitely not the mind of my infancy. There is just no accounting for my self as a discreet, enduring thing. In the end, it seems that my "self" amounts to nothing more than just a name given to the fleeting, ever-changing coalescence of body and mind as they pass through time and space.

The problem is that the natural sense of self that all beings possess by virtue of their sentiency has run along unexamined beneath our every experience in life, slowly growing into a monolithic pillar at the core of our identity. "She can't treat *me* that way!" "*I* deserve so much more." "Why does this have to happen to *me*?" We've grown attached to the sense that we are more than just complex mental and physical processes passing through this world. As a result, this self that is really nothing but a name for something that can't be pinned down has been blown completely out of proportion. Some are even willing to die or kill to protect their egos from assault.

Worst of all, clinging to the illusion that the unchanging self is real hurts us in the end. We cannot brook the slightest disrespect, or we crumple when things don't go the way we'd hoped. In overlooking the fleeting nature of our selves we've weakened and curtailed our own resiliency and ability to cope. This is why the Buddha's seemingly negative message that there is no self is actually a medicinal balm: embracing the fluctuating interdependent nature of our selves is not an end or extinction but the beginning of infinite possibility.

Our selves are not fixed. We are fluid, dimensioned, and potential. We only need let go of our ownership of the illusion of self.

Smile

Research has shown that a smile isn't just a nicety; it's an integral form of communication with others. Smiling is also an effective way to lift one's spirits. Neuroscientists have found that the networks in the brain associated with happiness are activated whenever we smile, regardless of whether the smile was really motivated by that feeling or was simply a performance. The mere act of smiling itself can prime the brain for happiness. Even if it's a completely mechanical smile, the brain doesn't seem to know the difference; it responds as if the smile were natural.

You may wonder why the brain is so gullible in the face of a faked smile. The answer lies in the mirror neuron system. One of the major challenges early humans faced long before we developed language and civilization was the challenge of determining the intentions of others. "How do I know if this person approaching is friend or foe?" Our amazing brains developed the capacity to read facial expressions and other bodily cues in strangers as a means of indicating "friend" or "foe." A network of neurons in the brain called the mirror neuron system reflects within us the information we detect from facial expressions and bodily cues in others. If a person smiles at us, our brain smiles back, and usually so does our face. The same system is at work when we instinctively flinch when we watch someone else crash their bicycle or get hit in the groin with a baseball on YouTube. It just so happens that when we make ourselves smile, even if we're simply imitating a real smile, the same network fires in the brain, providing us with a sense of ease, approachability, and happiness.

Buddha is usually depicted with a smile in statues and paintings. Usually a little half-smile that radiates peace. I advise my students sometimes to wear a little half-smile like the Buddha's when they practice. I particularly encourage it for walking meditation. Sometimes a smile arises naturally from the joy of practice. Other times, the imposed grin primes us to feel joy. Deportment has been given as a key element in meditation practice since the time of the Buddha. We intuitively know that the way we carry ourselves affects our minds. We keep our backs upright and straight, shoulders level, and legs placed so that they give our posture sturdiness. I see no problem with adding the element of a gentle smile to this regimen of postural advice, in order to bring a little joy to the sitting.

The principal indicator that I'm drifting into storytelling during meditation is tension in my jaw. My jaw tends to clench when I drift away from the moment at hand to worry about the future or regret the past. If I make holding a gentle smile a part of my meditative deportment, it makes it much easier to notice when tension has crept into my face, and thereby easier to notice when I have grown distracted. The combination of the pleasant feeling of releasing tension and the pleasant feeling of smiling really buoys the practice. Holding a gentle smile is a good way to train positive feelings and is also a good way to remain mindful about one's thoughts as they are expressed in the body.

Children smile about four hundred times a day. By the time we have grown into adulthood, we don't smile anywhere near that much. Imagine how different we might feel if we did. Add to your meditative posture the practice of holding a little smile on your lips. When you're done with your practice and going about your daily business, remember to smile, whether just to yourself or sharing it with someone else. You may find that happiness comes a little bit easier if you do.

If you are not smiling now, give it a try. ☺

Stress

Stress has gotten a pretty bad name. But stress actually performs a vital function in life: it motivates us to take action when under threat, whether that threat is an immediate physical threat like a tiger or a situational threat like losing one's job. Stress really only becomes problematic when we let it spin out of control to become a default mental state, even in the absence of any real threat. So the key to managing stress isn't to eradicate it altogether but to restrict it to those situations in which it is actually useful.

Mindfulness has come to prominence lately as a very effective means of regulating stress. A solid body of research, built up over the past thirty-five years, has established that mindfulness meditation is an effective intervention for regulating stress, even stress related to physical pain, such as recovery from medical procedures or injury. But just as we shouldn't carry our negative assessments of stress to an extreme, we must also be careful to keep our positive assessments of mindfulness anchored to reality. Mindfulness is not a cure-all. It can have beneficial effects in terms of stress management, but there are often complex causes for stress, and mindfulness alone may not be the solution in every case.

Years ago I bought a car that came with traction control. At the time traction control—the automatic computerized application of breaking and steering to maneuver the car safely out of a skid—was an innovative technology. The user's manual made a point of saying that, while the technology was great, it could not undo the laws of physics; if the car went into a skid at a sufficient speed and with too much momentum, traction control would not be able to correct it. Likewise, mindfulness can help us regulate stress, but given conditions extreme enough, there is little that mindfulness alone could accomplish. So the best use for mindfulness in terms of regulating stress is in those situations wherein the stress can actually be regulated.

To begin with, we must learn to build the general cognitive skill of being able to recognize when we begin to engage in a self-narrative that is likely to produce stress. Mark Twain once said, "I've been through some terrible things in my life, some of which actually happened." Sometimes we put ourselves through hell by following fantasies and stories of how bad things were, are, or will be, despite the fact that there is actually no immediately actionable stressor present. If we allow ourselves to be caught in cycles of thought like this, we may end up slipping into a state of enduring stress. Seeking relief in food, alcohol, and other short-term and unhealthy distractors only compounds the problem. If we can recognize this cycle when it's just being set in motion, our practice of mindfulness has a better chance of nipping it in the bud.

- When you recognize the onset of a cycle of stressful thought, set aside a few minutes to meet this cycle in meditation. If you are traveling or working, find a quiet corner or secluded spot where you can safely spend a few minutes without interruption.
- Settle your body and mind by sitting comfortably in an alert posture and following the breath for a few cycles.
- When you feel gathered and ready to confront your stress, begin by examining the nature of the trigger: is the stressor an immediate, real, and tangible problem? If it is, take a moment to acknowledge it, put aside the various narratives about how terrible it is, how you might fail to overcome it, and so on. Real problems are better than imagined ones because there is actually something you can do about them. Reassure yourself that you can handle it. This isn't just cheerleading; you have handled countless problems successfully throughout your life, although you may not have given yourself credit for them.
- Is the stressor an imagined, speculative, or distant problem? If it is, take a moment to acknowledge the nature of the

stressor, particularly its relative abstraction and distance. As you did for "real" problems, put aside the various narratives about how terrible it will be, how you might fail to overcome it, and remind yourself that it is only a possibility. For the moment you have the capacity to choose paths than may have different outcomes. Do not be afraid.

- Sit with your stress, grounding your mind in the moment, in the bodily sensation of your breath moving in and out of your lungs, and move away from extraneous storytelling about the problem at hand. Feel the sensations of the stress as they register in your body.
- Continue to breathe and practice the gentle return for as long as you need to relieve the immediate sense of stress.

Early intervention in the cycle of negative thought can avert the build-up of stress. In order to successfully intervene at an early stage, we must cultivate the broader cognitive skill of recognizing negative cycles of thought when they begin. Eventually, with practice, when you notice the mental and physical signatures of stress, you will be able to simply note them and let them go. "Stress." "Anxiety." "Tension." And then gently return the mind to a healthier mental or physical object of observation. Acknowledgment undermines the power of stress and redirection allows us to choose a healthier train of thought for ourselves. When used properly, mindfulness can help us to correct out of a skid into unneeded stress.

Sympathetic Joy

"Congratulations! I am so happy for you!" Sympathetic joy is the genuine feeling that "your happiness is my happiness"; it is the ability to rejoice in the success of others. I use "sympathetic joy" to translate the Pali word *mudita*, but we might also translate this word as "tender hearted." In Buddhism, sympathetic joy is considered one of the four Brahmaviharas, or "pure abodes." A person who embraces sympathetic joy and the three other pure abodes—compassion, loving-kindness, and equanimity—accomplishes the greatest good.

When we are truly able to rejoice in the successes of others, without feelings of competitiveness, jealousy, or resentment, we are expressing pure sympathetic joy. The joy that others experience begets joy in us. In this way, sympathetic joy also taps into our natural understanding of the principle of interconnectedness. There is enough happiness for everyone. We needn't worry that being happy for the successes of others might somehow diminish our own happiness. You will find that the more you allow yourself to express natural feelings of joy, the more available joy becomes to you.

It may come as a surprise that getting in touch with natural feelings of happiness for others happens largely by letting go of attachment to ourselves. This is one of the core ideas at the heart of Buddhist life for good reason. Detachment from our egos or our "selves" opens us up to a greater sense of empathy. Although some people get the wrong idea from the constant Buddhist message of nonattachment, thinking that anyone who pursues such a path in life must be cold, distant, and aloof, actually, this sense of nonattachment to the ego is what gives Buddhists a reputation for being cheerful and resilient people. Our sense of well-being need not be contingent upon our own private success or gain when, through a greater sense of connectedness with others, we can genuinely share in the joy of their successes.

Inserting the practice of cultivating sympathetic joy into our daily routine once in a while is a way to warm up our practice of mindfulness:

- Begin, as always, by finding and settling the mind on your breath. Take a few moments to settle yourself before you turn your mind to the practice of sympathetic joy.
- First, reflect on your own personal situation as a living being: we all naturally wish to be happy and desire success in our

endeavors. Reflect on your own humanity and develop a warm sense of regard for yourself.

- Now extend this reflection to those friends and family and immediate relations. They, like you, genuinely wish to be happy and to find success in life. Reflect on this and develop a sense of warm heartedness for them.
- Lastly, extend your reflection to all living beings, encompassing all people and animals in the world. All of us, although we do not know one another, share in common this desire to be happy and successful.
- Spend a few moments thinking about how wonderful it would be if we all could achieve our goals, find happiness, and take joy in it.
- Sit with the feeling of sympathetic joy that you raise as long as you like.

The more we prime ourselves to take joy in the happiness and success of others, the more likely that feeling will naturally arise as we encounter such in life. Wonderful!

Thought

We are hooked on thinking. The large cerebral cortex that we carry around in our skulls predisposes us to thinking. I do it from the moment I get up in the morning until I hit the pillow at night (and then for some time after). When my penchant for thought is at its worst, I plan my day obsessively, reviewing the sequence of events and rehearsing conversations, most of which will never occur in the way that I imagine. Sometimes thoughts repeat as if on a loop. A short session of meditation helps me interrupt the loop of thoughts when I catch myself ruminating, but I know mindfulness will never do away with thought altogether.

The purpose of meditation is not to get rid of thoughts. Neither is it to suppress them. If thoughtlessness is your goal, better to try sedation! It is natural that we human beings think, and much of the time thought is productive and useful. The aim of meditation is to develop a better relationship with our thoughts, to see when they are and when they aren't beneficial. Meditation helps us to think skillfully.

By "thoughts" we're referring broadly to the activity of the mind, including inner verbal monologue, images that arise in the mind's eye, and emotions. We can distinguish two general categories of thought: automatic and deliberate. The default mode of thought is an ongoing internal monologue, or imagined dialogues, carried on without much awareness. This mode of thought is automatic. Deliberate thoughts are directed and we are aware of them. Deliberate thoughts require intention. Deliberate thought can lead to scientific discovery, artistic creation, or even spiritual liberation, but it also leads to the invention of weapons of mass destruction, organized war, and systematic atrocities. It is vitally important that we human beings be able to distinguish between useful and harmful thoughts.

To begin with, we must recognize thoughts as thoughts. This means that we will need to spend time bringing awareness to bear on our default mode of thinking. We must notice when our mind has become lost in thought, unconsciously weaving a narrative about this or that, lost in storytelling. With a regular practice of mindfulness, you will find that it is much easier to notice when you've become lost in thought. Once you recognize that you've been meandering through a story, simply note the story for what it is, and return your attention to the task immediately at hand: if you are walking focus on walking, if you are cooking focus on the process of preparing the food, if you are listening to a friend give her your full attention. Learning to implement mindfulness in this way helps us to be generally more present in our lives.

Now we must work on evaluating the usefulness of the thoughts we think or the lines of thinking that we choose to follow. I may begin to think about someone I am having difficulty with, for example. My mind soon finds itself building a complete record of all the reasons that this person is unlikeable: the insulting things they've said, their discourteous behavior, their lack of taste in music. Before long this string of thoughts recruits anger, and I'm ready to mount a full-scale mental attack on the character of my soon-to-be enemy. When I recognize that my thoughts are directed along these lines that bear useless results, I can choose to intervene. Noticing the angry tone of my thoughts about this person, I could choose instead to do some perspective taking or recontextualization: "Well, he's only human. Like most of us he struggles with his own issues and sometimes acts regrettably, but deep inside he only wants to find happiness like I do." This is a more useful tack.

Learning to distinguish good thoughts from bad is the first step to freeing ourselves from the trap of negative thinking. Given the force of habit behind the thoughts we normally think, it will be difficult to change ourselves right away. Mindfulness, again, provides us with techniques that prove useful in this respect. Those thought-habits that are attractive or difficult to undo, such as thinking about how disagreeable some people are, need simply be noted as "thought." If we cannot reverse them, for the time being we can simply note that they occur and return our focus to the breath or the task at hand. Thoughts will inevitably arise; our task is to recognize their presence and to redirect attention to something that is actually happening in the present moment.

A lifetime of conditioning will not evaporate with a single act of effort. It takes time to change the way we think. The goal is not to eliminate thoughts but to redirect our attention away from unskillful thoughts, and eventually to choose beneficial thoughts instead of harmful ones, when we do think.

Time

There is a charming exchange between Pooh and Piglet in A. A. Milne's memorable *Winnie the Pooh* books:

> "What day is it?" asked Pooh.
> "It's today," squeaked Piglet.
> "My favorite day," said Pooh.

If we asked Pooh what time it was, he might say, "Now." It's always now, whether we are paying attention to that fact or not. Sometimes now is just a concept. We spread the concept of now across many succeeding moments, imagining them all to be one big now, and then we elaborate on our feelings about this "now." "I like this . . ." or "I don't like this." The actual now is experienced directly when we let conceptual elaboration fall away and rest in the fleetingness of the moment.

Our sense of time depends on how we pay attention to the moments of our lives. We usually understand time in terms of an imagined future and the remembered past. Our subjective feeling of time springs from the tension between ourselves and our pasts and futures. If we give up dragging along the past and reaching for the future, time loses its shoes. In the moment, there is just experience, and this experience is timeless amd walks barefoot in the present.

The present moment is the principal commodity of attention. Our moments can be experienced fully or squandered through distraction. We may miss more than just these moments. We may lose hours, days, months, and years, perhaps a lifetime. It is possible to live most of our lives distracted by the next pressing thing on our to-do list: getting the kids to school, sending them off to college, getting them married, and tending to the grandchildren. The march of time is unrelenting and that force can sweep us along if we don't have a space where we can step out of time.

A solid meditation practice provides us glimpses of timelessness and allows us to pull back from the frantic distractedness of life. We discover that time is subjective, plastic, and that we have some degree of control over it. One evening during a meditation retreat at a Zen temple, the hour between the bell that began the session and the bell that ended it flew by in what seemed to be a matter of minutes, so much so that I thought the session had been cut short. When I examined what I had done to make time pass in this way, I realized that I had given myself wholly over to the moment. I stopped marking time by wandering to the future and past, and the ongoing commentary about the present had grown completely quiet. Dropping the concept of now and resting in the actual now, I had stepped outside of the normal everyday experience of time.

Time is only meaningful when we don't have enough of it, when we feel rushed, harried, and burdened by that tyrannical to-do list. That pressured sense of time pushes us away from the actual present. Here in the actual now anxiety has no purchase. A man who suffered a stroke experienced a sense of timelessness: "I had lost the ability to converse with others. . . . and to engage in self-talk. In other words, I did not have the ability to think about the future—to worry, to anticipate or perceive it—at least not with words. Thus, for the first four or five weeks after hospitalization, I simply existed."

The experience of timelessness is available to any of us each time we let go of the past, the present, and the future, and lose ourselves in the moment.

Tolerance

I was at a black- tie event, a thank-you fete for donors to the University of Vermont and other VIPs. At my table was a large man in a cheap suit, loud tie, and white sneakers. I thought to myself, "Who is this joker?" I couldn't imagine why *he* was at this event. As the evening unfolded, he was charming, affable, and gregarious, and I learned that he had donated millions to the university—orders of magnitude more than my small contribution. At first, I was astonished and then embarrassed by my hasty stereotyping of this man. He turned out to be a wonderful person, not resembling my first impression at all.

When a situation feels intolerable we often find ourselves thinking, "I can't stand this!" Whether we can't stand to deal with a person or we can't stand some situation, intolerance boils down to not being able to accept what we do not want. But the reality is that sometimes what we do not want is just the way it is. In order to spare ourselves from further misery and pain, sometimes we must simply endure hardship. Tolerance allows us to face, with equanimity, the problems we hoped never to experience. Tolerance is by definition the ability to remain unaffected by circumstances. Of course, tolerance is usefully applied when facing difficulties that are unavoidable. We can always close the window when we are cold, but we can't simply close the window on the sadness of a breakup or the grief of losing a loved one. These are times in which we must be prepared to endure the unpleasant.

The practice of mindfulness trains our minds to be more objective about what we can and cannot change. Our untrained impulse is to elaborate on our displeasure when encountering hardship. "This sucks! Why is this happening to me now? I don't deserve this. Of course it would have to be today!" If we are able to look at the situation clearheadedly, we should quickly be able to judge whether we can do anything to change it or whether it is simply something we must experience whether or not we want to. Tolerance allows us to bear what we must without making it worse for ourselves by ruminating on it. Surprisingly, you will find that if you relieve yourself of the mental chatter that typically follows on unpleasant experiences, the experiences no longer seem as difficult to bear.

One of the ways in which we can train tolerance in our daily practice is to deal with the physical discomfort of sitting:

- Once you have settled into your posture and entered your practice, be on the lookout for physical discomfort and its attendant narrative.

- When you experience pain in your legs, for example, rather than elaborate on this pain by returning again and again to your displeasure with it, focus instead on the bare sense of the pain itself.

- If you sit with the pain long enough, it begins to decompose into components. There may be a warmth to it, a pulsing sensation, or a prickly, tingling sensation. Look into the pain to see what it's made of.

- When the mind begins to offer suggestions about how to avoid this pain ("Maybe I could shift my posture. Maybe I could unfold my legs."), simply note this escape-seeking mind and return to the meditation at hand, at least for a while.

- Sitting in any posture for a prolonged period leads to discomfort. If we shifted our seats every time we felt a slight discomfort, we would be as fidgety as first graders! Learning to relate to normal levels of discomfort can facilitate our progress.

Of course, in order to use physical discomfort as a basis for developing tolerance, you must first have a healthy relationship to your body, with flexibility and knowing your limits where discomfort turns into injury. Tolerance doesn't mean to harm yourself in a bid to see how far you can take something. The goal is to know when your mind is simply seeking to escape temporary discomfort and when there is a legitimate need to move.

Uncertainty

When I was in high school, in the depths of the Cold War, it seemed as if the destruction of the world was imminent. There was a seemingly boundless proliferation of nuclear weapons, each new weapon capable of destroying an even more unimaginable number of lives than the last. The policy of the day was Mutually Assured Destruction (MAD). As the acronym suggests, it was as if the superpowers were mad with the ambition to outdo one another in terms of destructive capacity.

At the time we were reading existentialist authors like Victor Frankl and Albert Camus in school. Our teacher reminded me that people have always felt an unsettling sense of uncertainty living in the world. The rise of Nazi Germany and the Holocaust cast a bleak shadow over the world of Frankl and Camus. In earlier eras of European history, the invading Huns were like a black pall on the horizon. In the face of an ever-changing world humans have always longed to feel secure.

But life is as uncertain today as it was thousands of years ago. A good deal of what the Buddha taught revolves around the fact that life is uncertain. As uncomfortable as it may seem, uncertainty is the bedrock of our reality—everything is always changing. No matter how hard we may try to aim for certainty of outcome, in the end we have to admit that we just never really know what will happen next. The Buddha's approach to this problem was not to push against reality in an attempt to shape it to our desired state but to learn to recognize reality and adapt our minds to work in harmony with it. If we cling to an expectation of a certain outcome, we set ourselves up to suffer all the more if it doesn't happen. We must learn to accept uncertainty and to approach our lives with that reality in mind.

Performance artist Janine Antoni taught herself to walk a tightrope. She comments that her mastery of the skill came not when she knew how to balance perfectly but when she developed a better understanding of imbalance. Rather than overcompensate when the rope shifted under her feet, Antoni learned to adapt to the motion and remain atop the rope. We can approach uncertainty in the same way. Rather than overreact to the vicissitudes of our daily fortunes, with the knowledge that nothing is certain anyway, we can more easily adapt to changing situations. The taming of our overreactive minds allows us a bit of comfort, even in the face of uncertainty.

No amount of fame and fortune can protect us from the unexpected and unwanted incidents of life. While wealth can purchase better health care and face-lifts, it won't grant immunity from sickness and aging. The most powerful CEOs may be able to influence the political landscape, but even they cannot guarantee that the laws they want will be passed. We just don't know what is going to happen.

We all live on borrowed time and may even be one breath away from our last. Uncertainty doesn't have to be an occasion for cynicism. An awareness of the nature of change makes the sweet moments in life all the sweeter. Knowing that life is uncertain imbues our experiences with poignancy: the value of moments spent with friends and loved ones becomes very clear. Uncertainty can teach us to slow down and appreciate what we have, rather than focusing on what we lack.

Vipassana

Much of what we practice as mindfulness meditation today derives from the ancient Buddhist discipline of *vipassana* or "insight meditation." Vipassana is practiced in almost every Buddhist tradition, but the form of vipassana most widely known in the world comes from the Theravada Buddhist tradition. The practice of vipassana preserved in the Theravada tradition is said to be the form of insight meditation taught and practiced by the Buddha himself.

I sat my first vipassana retreat in the summer of 1989. It was the single most difficult *and* valuable experience of my life. It was ten days punctuated by torture, bliss, breakthroughs, and deep states of concentration. Emerging from that course, I was changed. I lived inside my skin in a different way. I meditated every day. I was fully engaged with my schoolwork. I felt clear, as I never had before. Of course that clarity faded over time, but some of it stayed with me and has been nurtured by subsequent practice and retreats.

The practice of vipassana, as its name suggests, produces insight. What is this insight that it produces? It is a deep penetration into our own natures gained by observing the simplest aspects of our being. Since most meditators first learn to calm the mind by focusing on the breath, the breath also tends to become the first object of insight meditation by default. Insight meditation, rather than taking the breath as an anchor to produce concentration, begins to investigate the quality of the breath itself. We begin to notice the movement of the breath, the many different moments of a single inhale, the various different bodily sensations that accompany the breath, and how the mind is tied up to these sensations. Close and sustained investigation of something as simple as the process of breathing leads us to clearly see the body and mind as a ceaseless flux of changing physical and mental components. Insight meditation brings impermanence directly into our awareness. This kind of direct perception of the impermanent nature of our being has the power to transform our experience and behavior long after our session has ended.

As our practice of vipassana progresses, we begin to see how the way in which our minds relate to events and experiences doesn't really jibe with their fleeting nature. We tend to cling to those moments that are pleasant and are saddened when they pass. We mentally squirm in the face of unpleasant experiences, hoping that they will hurry up and end. Our natural tendency is to treat our experiences as more enduring, stable, and real than they really are. We add a layer of frustration to our experience in life by pushing and pulling against experiences as they arise. Our mental pushing and pulling drags us into the past ("Not this again!") or into the future ("I hope this will last!"), taking us away from the reality that is unfolding in the moment. These mental contortions trail fear in their wake—the fear of meeting what we don't want and losing what we do want.

The insight that much of our suffering comes from fear of change leads us to examine the agent of this fear. Who is the "I" that feels so tossed about and beaten by the ever-changing circumstances in which we find ourselves? Whatever this "I" is, it seems to emerge from the flux of mental and physical events I think of as my "self." But when delved into, no single component of this flux, nor all of them together, can be identified as the "self" I feel so invested in protecting. The "self" is merely a projection onto the ceaseless flow of physical and mental experience that comprises the continuum of my life. Ultimately, when we let go of clinging to this "self," we find rest, peace, and deep, abiding happiness, even in the midst of constant change.

For most, the practice of vipassana is quite an intense experience. But with a solid daily practice of mindfulness as a foundation, vipassana is much less difficult to engage in and master. The practice of mindfulness itself combines elements of both shamatha, or "serenity meditation" to develop concentration, and vipassana, or "insight meditation" that leads to transformative penetration of the nature of reality. When you are ready to bring your mindfulness practice to the next level, look into joining a vipassana retreat led by a skilled teacher.

Visitation

Late one evening as I was driving home from work, exhausted at the end of a long week, a memory paid me a visit. I recalled an internship interview I had had at a prestigious hospital in Boston. I flubbed a question with the director of the hospital that probably cost me the job offer. Turning this thought over in my mind, I began to feel that this event, now nearly twenty years ago, had ruined my career. In my exhausted state, that conclusion felt very real, and compelling, despite the fact that my career has been just fine. Sometimes memories of past failures or regrets come out of nowhere to pay us a visit. If we are unprepared for them, we may be ensnared in the stories they weave and cause ourselves grief.

Like specters out of the darkness, distant memories, thoughts, images, and emotions, whether wanted or unwanted, may visit us at any time. We can't control what comes to visit us, but we do have a say in how we handle the visit. When dark thoughts appear on the doorstep of our minds, their unbidden presence may unsettle us. It's easy to blow things out of proportion, or to fall into rumination on unpleasant past experiences. We all live with our failings, and we know that remembering them can be hard. But if we greet our unbidden visitors with mindfulness, we can note them simply as thoughts, or memories, or emotions, and let them pass through and be on their way. The key is to recognize these visitors for what they are, rather than becoming entangled in the content that they carry.

The Buddha said to invite your demons to tea. The wisdom of this notion comes down to acceptance. Memories are bound to visit us. Barring the door and mentally barricading ourselves against them only makes the situation worse. The Buddha encourages us to simply recognize our demons, "Oh, it's you! Have a seat and have a cup of tea." It is more skillful to greet our unhappy memories with acceptance, without resistance, but also without being swallowed up in them. Seeing the stories, worries, and "what if?" worst-case scenarios that come to us from time to time for what they are, we can treat them lightly. These visitations are like a happenstance encounter with an old lover while in transit at an airport in a different city: of course there is baggage there and just below the superficialities of the conversation lies an abyss of potential emotional and psychological entanglements. But neither of you go there because you are merely passing each other by. Understanding the fleeting nature of the encounter makes it possible to peacefully coexist with whatever is happening now.

When we don't focus on the whys and wherefores of remembered regrets, but simply accept them as momentary products of the mind, we shift our relationship to them. Identifying with or being swallowed up in painful memories creates distress. Mindfulness is the skill of extrication from unhealthy elaborative thought. We don't expect to extinguish the thoughts. When we extricate ourselves from the story, we can dissolve our attention into the moment-by-moment unfolding of experience, grounded in present bodily sensations, rather than in storytelling about the past or the future.

When we encounter childhood bullies as adults, the emotional charge and dominating power that their presence once held has faded. We may even greet them as childhood acquaintances and share a passing smile and hug on the street. Likewise, when approached with a mindful attitude, we can greet unpleasant memories from our past with recognition and a light touch. "Oh, I remember you! Have a seat. Have a cup of tea."

Vulnerability

A good part of walking the path of mindfulness is to be committed to vulnerability—to laying bare the nature of our minds and the fragility of being a living being in this world. According to the poet David Whyte, we have little hope of being authentic if we lack vulnerability. Our vulnerability—all our foibles, idiosyncrasies, miscues, and uncertainties—keep us working toward the possibility of awakening and allow us to laugh at ourselves along the way.

It seems that the meaning of vulnerability has gotten confused with weakness. Our extroverted culture powers itself on a veneer of invulnerability, perfection, and relentless ambition. "Go big or go home." There is no room for uncertainty, unpredictability, or instability. Nevertheless, the more we try to squeeze vulnerability out of our lives, the further from reality we get.

Mark Epstein points out in his eloquent *Trauma of Everyday Life* that the truth is that life is uncertain and filled with countless tiny traumas that come from having a body that is subject to sickness, old age, and death. Not to mention myriad other forms of loss. Everything is changing all the time but we like to pretend that things are stable or that they are under our control.

After the death of my beloved Rhodesian Ridgeback, Ruki, I adopted two rescue mutts, Harley and Sumi. We trail run just about every day and sometimes they take off on their own trajectory. They may start by chasing a rabbit, a fox, or who knows what, perhaps taking off to aggress the neighbor's chickens. One day they disappeared longer than usual and eventually returned with snouts full of porcupine quills. Sumi looked like a walrus with a symmetrical array of tusk-like whiskers jutting from her black muzzle. Harley had them as well, but longer and thicker and one of them lodged in his hard palate. Fortunately, it was nothing that $500 at the vet's office couldn't fix. Now each time they disappear, I wonder, "Will they get tangled up with another porcupine? Will they get stuck on a steep ledge (as Harley did recently)?

Will they get into some other, yet unimagined, trouble, like getting shot by the neighbor with the chickens?"

On a cold winter day, they disappeared again, this time into the Green Mountain Forest. While I was waiting for them, my mind was afire. I first thought about ways that I could better contain them. I had tried some treat training but it was obviously not enough. I needed a better solution. I decided that I would do something. I had taken an action with that decision. My mind had done a practical service. "Thank you." But my mind wanted to keep going. Even though I resolved whatever I could resolve in this moment, it wanted to keep thinking, ruminating, and generating fantasies. It was worried about the welfare of the dogs and it also had other complaints. I was cold and my companions were walking too slowly.

Some of these thoughts are a distraction from the unpleasant uncertainty surrounding the dogs' prolonged absence. I make another decision—I will try to move forward with mindfulness. First I must let go of the internal dialogues, then I must acknowledge the fact that even if the dogs were running by my side, I was still vulnerable to loss. Something could happen to any of us at any moment.

Now I started to breathe in all that uncertainty along with the five-degree air and breathe out a sense of equanimity. I could neither know nor, at this juncture, control what was happening. I walked this way for several minutes. I had already called to them and whistled. I could hear the echo of my efforts through the valley. I knew they heard me. They would come when they were ready. After about another fifteen minutes, they showed up out of breath and intact.

To love is to make ourselves vulnerable. To cherish something as I cherish the dogs is to make myself more vulnerable to the trauma of everyday life. In the end, vulnerability is about self-compassion. We have to acknowledge our limitations. We are not omniscient, perfect, and protected. We are whole, even though we are constantly subject to loss.

Walking

As I walk down the fifth fairway, I spy Mt. Mansfield, Vermont's tallest peak, looming in the distance, still covered with snow in early spring. The impeccable short mown grass is soft beneath my feet. I breathe, relaxed as I feel the sun warming my wind-blown face. My walk is a meditation. I am alone with my breath, the gentle movement of my limbs as I walk, and the sights, sounds, and smells that greet me this morning.

Walking is one of the four basic meditation postures that the Buddha prescribed, the others being sitting, standing, and lying down. There are of course very formal types of walking meditation, but if we are fortunate enough to have the capacity to walk, even an ordinary stroll can be the basis of our practice of mindfulness. We typically walk with some destination in mind. Walking meditation is a more deliberate kind of walking that focuses on the experience of walking itself, rather than on any destination. While doing walking meditation, the attention is placed on the breath, on the soles of the feet, other bodily sensations, or on the sights, sounds, and smells present in the landscape through which you walk.

Most of the time, we multitask while we walk—we think about work or social plans or we get lost listening to music or chatting on the phone. This kind of walking is automatic and unconscious. Given that we are already willing to allow ourselves to do other tasks while walking, why not make the walking itself a short session of mindfulness meditation? When walking from the car to the office, or from place to place at work, or when taking a stroll over our lunch break we can use the walk to practice mindfulness simply by bringing our full attention to the experience of walking.

- When walking somewhere, just walk.
- If you regularly walk down a corridor at work or home, designate it as a "thought-free zone," and mindfully focus on the experience of walking each time you walk there.
- When you are walking, bring your attention to the breath, the movement of the body, and other sensations.
- Let go of your to-do list for a few moments to enjoy some meditation.

Health experts recommend that we take ten thousand steps each day to maintain fitness. These ten thousand steps can contribute to our mental and spiritual health as well if we see them as opportunities to practice. Imagine the millions of steps you take as the months and years unfurl. Imagine what that can do for your awareness.

Witness

One day I was wearing my best suit because I was scheduled to give the keynote address at a conference later that evening. It was a sunny afternoon and I was walking my dog in downtown Burlington, Vermont, during my break, as I did every day. We walked by a group of young men. One of them looked my dog and me over and said, "Man, you look like a pimp!" For a fleeting moment I thought, "How dare you?!" Anger and indignation immediately began to rise. Instead of following these thoughts and emotions, I had to smile. I was able to step back from the chain of negative emotions that had been set in motion to witness the scene. Seeing what was happening, I said to myself, "No thanks." Being able to witness the workings of my mind allowed me to be dispassionate and to let it go.

Witnessing, like attention, is a trainable skill. The more we engage it, the more available it will be. We can choose to live our lives along two basic tracks: we can immerse ourselves in storytelling or we can focus on direct experience. It is quite common to get lost in constructing our own narratives: "He did this to me. I didn't deserve it. Nothing ever goes my way!" We may lose ourselves in memories of past events, daydreams about what we will do in the future, or rumination on the traits we presently possess. This kind of thinking tends to focus on "me" and leads to self-centered thought and behavior. If we can step back from ourselves, short-circuiting the constant self-centered narrative, we gain a bit of distance, we gain perspective. From a distance we can more objectively observe our thoughts and actions unfolding moment by moment. We begin to witness ourselves as we really are.

The distance available to us when we step back offers us the power to choose. If you can connect to the witness, you can move into your moment-by-moment process and make choices about where you want it to go:

- Settle yourself physically and mentally, find your breath, and begin your session of mindfulness.
- When distraction occurs and storytelling comes into play, rather than redirecting your awareness to the breath, begin to observe the narrative process itself.
- Narrative tends to move away from the present moment of experience, toward the past or the future. Witness how narrative uses imagination and daydream to do its work.
- Seeing that narrative acts based on withdrawal from the moment at hand, redirect your attention to the breath, to the sensations in your body, and to this particular moment of meditation. Observe whether storytelling continues or fades when you do this.

■ When storytelling abates, continue to practice with the breath. When distraction and storytelling occur again, repeat the process.

When you are able to observe the negative thoughts you are having as you obsess about the future, you can choose to think about things in a healthier way. By recognizing storytelling and turning from narrative to the experience at hand, you train your power to witness. The witness doesn't care if the process repeats; its job is to notice and to offer the choice to return. When we witness, we can participate more skillfully in our lives. We can have thoughts and we can also be aware that we are having the thoughts. Thoughts are just thoughts, even if they attempt to represent themselves as reality itself. Even though they may correlate with reality, thoughts are not the truth.

Wisdom

Wisdom isn't an intellectual affair, it's a lived experience. We may think of wisdom as something that we acquire, some tangible body of knowledge that we slowly accumulate over years of study. But wisdom isn't a "thing." It's more of an orientation or a way of being that influences and directs our thoughts, speech, and actions in the world. Some types of wisdom are commonplace, like knowing not to trust a "Nigerian prince" who emails to tell you that you can gain a fantastic sum if only you share with him your personal banking information. But some wisdom is profound. Some wisdom brings us into closer harmony with reality, which helps our ailing hearts to heal.

One of the ways that Buddhists think about wisdom is as a firm and incontrovertible understanding of existence marked in three ways: it is pervaded by suffering (or *dukkha*), is in a constant state of change, and is without any essential "self" at its core. Understanding these three marks changes the way we move through the world. All living beings are plagued by a constant sense of unease; suffering is always lurking close at hand. We strive to find happiness, but we know deep down that worldly happiness will fade: our new girlfriend or boyfriend may leave us, we may grow bored and dissatisfied with the current sporting trends we so passionately engage in today, our bodies grow old and breakdown. Seeing that dissatisfaction and change mark existence lessens our attachment to lovers, property (including our bodies), and activity from the very beginning. When a lover moves on, wisdom makes it easier to let go. The pain of separation itself indicates the reality of our existence, thereby deepening our wisdom.

A firm grasp of the fact that there is no essential self at the heart of our existence frees us from the misery of self-absorption. Everything that doesn't go my way doesn't have to be about me. The "I" to which we ordinarily cling when feeling disrespected, humiliated, or victimized loses its motivating power. Angry words, bitter recriminations, or passive-aggressive acts leveled against us fall like snowflakes rather than bomb blasts when we let go of our "selves." The eye of wisdom allows us to see these things from a different perspective: causes and conditions are ever at work behind the events we experience in life, and blame and anger find no foothold in the endless web of interconnected karmas. Things are what they are, and we must keep our cool in order to end the cycle of negativity. This is wisdom.

How do we come to this wisdom? If you have taken up a daily practice of mindfulness, you are already well on your way. We cultivate wisdom by quieting our normally chattering minds and attending squarely to the reality of our experience, beginning with something simple and easy to observe, like the breath. As the mind grows calm and our observation more acute, we begin to recognize the marks of existence. Yes, the breath is always changing: in through the nose, down to the lungs, and out through the nose, again and again, but each time is different. Discomfort comes and goes but always waits to reemerge. Ah, the more I focus on myself and how I dislike a sensation, the more painful it grows. When I let myself go, poof! It's as if it never happened.

First in the lab of our little meditation sessions, we experiment with seeing things clearly. As time wears on our repeated observations grow into wisdom. Little by little we notice that our way of being has changed: a little calmer, a little easier going, more forgiving. This is wisdom at work. Keep your practice and cherish the little changes.

May you grow ever wiser!

Xanax

Xanax is the brand name for alprazolam, an antianxiety drug. Xanax is just the latest successor in a parade of drugs meant to cure anxiety: first came Valium and Librium, Serax, Ativan, and Klonopin, then came Prozac, Zoloft, Lexapro, followed by Celexa, Paxil, and Cymbalta. What is truly amazing is that you likely recognize more than a few of these names. We seem to be living in the age of anxiety. Diagnoses of anxiety problems, along with depression, are on the rise. Tens of millions of prescriptions for antianxiety drugs and antidepressant drugs are written, and filled, every year.

Anxiety and stress are real problems that human beings have had to deal with since time immemorial. The great difference in the modern world is that the source of our anxiety tends to be internal rumination rather than external predators or environmental dangers. We are learning how to recognize and cope with the anxiety that comes with negative, self-critical inner monologue. Our society has struggled to find ways of coping with self-inflicted stress. In the twentieth century advancements in our understanding of the brain and the biological components of psychological states made medicating such problems seem like a promising solution. However, as time has worn on, it seems quite apparent that pills are not a cure-all. To truly heal our internal ills, techniques that allow us to have greater control over the unfolding of stress are needed.

Decades of research have demonstrated that mindfulness-based interventions and mindfulness meditation can reduce distress, anxiety, and depression. In some situations mindfulness practice alone is capable of resolving anxiety. In other cases, such as when one has been diagnosed with a clinical condition, mindfulness can be combined with medications. This is a decision that your physician and mental health provider must make with you. The take-home message is that mindfulness is a beneficial supplement to most treatments for anxiety, and regular practice of mindfulness is known to prevent reoccurrence of problems.

Mindfulness is also helpful for dealing with everyday bouts of anxiety:

- When you feel anxiety setting in, make a conscious decision to face it mindfully.
- Settle into your body and mind, find your breath, and rest your focus on it as you inhale and exhale.
- Shift your attention away from the mental storyline that is feeding your anxiety to focus on what is happening in the body instead.
- Is there tightness in the jaw, neck, or shoulders, or disquieting sensations in the gut? Focus on the breath as it moves in and out of your lungs, letting go of the tension in the body with each exhale.
- When the anxiety narrative reasserts itself, simply note it, and return your attention to the breath.
- Continue until the body and the mind feel sufficiently relaxed, and the anxiety has abated or feels less distressing.

Notice what happens when you give yourself permission to disconnect from the storylines that were driving the anxiety. As with many psychological stressors, the root lies in unchecked rumination. Unless anxious thoughts are driving helpful actions, they are not helping us. A good rule to follow regarding anxious thoughts is that they are useful if they lead to some practical action that resolves anxiety, but they are not useful if they do not. This rubric can be used to deal with all kinds of anxieties.

No prescription required.

Yoga

I practice yoga every day. It connects me to my body and provides me the flexibility to stably assume a cross-legged meditation posture. Most people know yoga as a practice of assuming physical postures called asanas. What people may not know is that the purpose of the yoga postures is to prepare the body for meditation.

In ancient India "yoga" was synonymous with what we think of today as "meditation." The Buddha was actually a prodigious yogi. At the beginning of his spiritual career he spent six years mastering the yogas of his day, studying with advanced gurus and developing his skill on his own. In the end he found the techniques available insufficient in his quest to end suffering and ended up forging a whole new path that combined traditional yoga with his radical new view of "no-self" or "selflessness."

So the practice of yoga is not contradictory to the practice of Buddhism. Like any other activity, yoga can be practiced mindfully, engaging your full attention. It is not just the activity but how we engage in the activity that allows it to be a part of our practice of mindfulness. It's not the postures themselves. We can do a perfect pose and be mentally lost in daydreams or fantasies, a million miles away from the practice itself. Done in this way, yoga becomes just another form of exercise that we can check out on, like running on a treadmill. But done mindfully, yoga can be an aid to self-transformation and enlightenment.

If you practice yoga, use the postures as an opportunity to practice mindfulness. As you move into the postures and hold them, move away from preoccupation with the abstract "you" to the concrete experience of the body as it stretches, folds, and holds energy. Push your mind forward into the frontier of embodied experience to explore the dialectic between fear and ego. If you characteristically shy away from discomfort, challenge, and uncertainty, then lean further into the posture. If you characteristically push yourself beyond your limits, perhaps to impress others, explore the gentleness of holding back. The challenge of holding precise, difficult-to-hold postures offers a rich field of sensations to concentrate upon. Focusing on this tension will take you from self-consciousness and is a readily available place to return the attention to when your mind wanders.

Since we spend much of our day in motion, bringing mindfulness to yogic movement can create a bridge to everyday activities. With sufficient practice, mindfulness can help us to know the difference between pushing too hard and not pushing hard enough to master particular postures. Practicing yoga mindfully can help us develop our senses of interoception and proprioception—awareness of the physiological condition of the body and of the relationship of parts of the body to each other, respectively. The mindful practice of yoga contributes to the development of a type of bodily wisdom that can aid us in all areas of our lives.

Zafu

While it is possible to meditate anywhere under any conditions, it helps to have the proper gear. A *zafu* is a circular cushion filled with cotton batting called *kapok* or buckwheat hulls (I prefer the buckwheat hulls—they are firm, but they have a little spring to them). Zafus come in different sizes; taller ones are better for those who are less flexible.

The zafu is typically placed on a *zabuton*, which is a flat, rectangular, mat-like cushion that comfortably supports the folded legs. This is the basic set-up for seated meditation. Some people place other objects in their meditation area that inspire or support their practice. I keep a modest statue of the Buddha in my meditation space to remind me of the Buddha within—my own potential for awakening. I usually light incense and a candle when I practice as well. I use a small hand bell and the timer on my phone to mark the beginning and end of my sessions. The idea is to sensibly use whatever supports your practice. Remember not to get carried away with accoutrements but to choose them wisely as aids to practice. Remember: cushions, incense, and bells, while helpful, won't do the practice for you.

Of course, it isn't absolutely necessary to sit cross-legged on the floor either. We can wake up just as well sitting in a chair, doing walking meditation, or even standing on our heads! Having a dedicated space for practice can facilitate your practice. Ideally, you will be able to set aside a room in your home or a corner of a room to use just for sitting. Reserving such a space announces to everyone, including yourself, that you take the practice seriously enough to devote some precious real estate to it. A dedicated meditation space also acts as a daily reminder to practice. As you spend more and more time practicing in your meditation space, the place itself becomes a subtle cue that reinforces the desire and commitment to practice.

The zafu and the practice space create a container for practice. Sitting on a cushion allows one to remain comfortably seated for longer periods of time. Sitting in a cross-legged posture provides a structural stability to the body that encourages a steady practice. If you are not naturally very flexible, there are yoga practices you can pursue that will help you to open your hips so you can sit on the zafu more comfortably. While the zafu won't do the work for you, it does provide a comfortable setting that makes practice more inviting.

The presence of the zafu proclaims a commitment to practice. It sits and waits for you to sit upon it. Like the breath, it waits without complaint. It doesn't say, "You never call! You never write!" It is there as a silent invitation to practice.

Are you ready to answer?

Afterword

Each of the A–Z facets forms the diamond of an awakened life. If you can understand, embrace, and put these facets of wisdom into practice, you will move toward awakening. It's really not moving *toward* in the sense of a destination. Awakening is right here and right now. Through insight and practice, moments of awakening follow, coming out of the matrix of goodness that you embody in the world.

You can test these truths for yourself. Nothing in this book requires faith in something unseen or something outside of you. Wisdom lives in the present moment and you participate in making the world what it is. Awakening starts with your individual mind and spreads out in the matrix of interactions with everything around you. You make these efforts, not because you "should," but rather due to the wonderful feeling of rightness that arises when you bring mindfulness to your life.

This book presents the "essential" teachings of a system that has no "essences"—no *things* that stand outside of the constant *becoming* of experience. No essences are required for awakening. It is here—always and now.

If you have read each of the 108 entries, you have had a taste of the Buddha's revolutionary teachings and their main expression through the cultivation of mindfulness. Mindfulness is a practice developed in the ordinary moments of life. There is nothing esoteric about the Buddha's teaching—the dharma. Mindfulness is the clear expression of living now.

There are no shortcuts in life, although selling shortcuts is good for business. We are out of touch with ourselves, out of rhythm with the daily cycles of life. Yet these cycles can be reclaimed in any moment when we remember to touch the rhythm of breathing. It's not a trick. Mindfulness is both natural and unnatural. We need to set aside some deeply conditioned habits to be awake. Biology undergirds some of these habits. Culture provides others. Yet somewhere in the midst of these conditionings is the sense of just being. We stumble upon this *beingness* from time to time, but most of the time it remains out of reach. Practicing mindfulness and embracing the Buddha's Dharma makes this beingness available in any moment, in fact, *every* moment of our lives.

It is right here, right now, without exception. No moment is exempt. This moment is a moment to awaken. Notice your breathing; notice the world around you; notice how you are a part of everything. This is your natural state. You don't have to transcend anything other than the limited ideas you hold about yourself. You can let go of this fiction and when it comes back you can let go of it again. You can find your home now.

On a recent trip to Charlotte, North Carolina, I walked into the lobby of a skyscraper. A sign said "No weapons." I was carrying my laptop that has a "love" sticker on it (from the Love postage stamps). George Orwell said, "In times of universal deceit, telling the truth becomes a revolutionary act." I remarked to myself that this laptop is a "weapon" that registers words of "truth." The manuscript it contains is part of a revolutionary act that started 2,500 years ago. The Buddha's teachings are just as radical and just as necessary today. The Buddha's message is, at its most practical, a message of love.

On my flight to Charlotte, I noticed a German man sitting across from me a row behind. I overhear him complain that he has nothing to read for the flight. I was reading Andrew Olendzki's *Unlimiting Mind: The Radically Experiential Psychology of Buddhism,* so I offer him my copy. He accepts it eagerly. I keep checking back to see how he is doing. I half expect him to give up on the text but, no, he is riveted. An hour and counting and he hasn't strayed from the book. At the end of the flight he's studied twenty-seven pages. He reaches out his hand and we shake for a long minute. His gratitude is heartening. The

Buddha's teachings are about transformation. A seed of revolution was planted that evening.

I'm flying home a few days later, and the man and I are on the same flight again! I hand him my copy of *Unlimiting Mind* so he can resume reading. The seeds have sprouted. He's now considering meditation. Perhaps later this day, and in the days to come, there will be a little more goodness in the world.

Acknowledgments

The writing of a book, like so many things in life, is influenced by many lives and acts of goodness. I am grateful to Josh Bartok at Wisdom Publications for his faith in this project. I am also indebted to the tireless work of Andy Francis, my editor, who has taken a deep interest in this project and has gone above and beyond what most editors are required to do in the preparation of a manuscript. My dharma friend Mu Soeng remains a constant source of support and inspiration. Much appreciation goes to the writer and my meditation student Louella Bryant for her edits of earlier versions of this manuscript. As always, I am aware of the students I teach and those I reach through my writing. Without them, there would be no point to writing. I am also appreciative of the lessons I've learned about the Buddha, the Abihdamma, and secular Buddhism from Andrew Olendzki.

About the Author

 Arnie Kozak is a clinical assistant professor in the Department of Psychiatry at the University of Vermont College of Medicine and a licensed psychologist–doctorate in the state of Vermont. He is a workshop leader at the Barre Center for Buddhist Studies, Kripalu Center for Yoga and Health, and the Copper Beech Institute. He is the author of multiple books including *Wild Chickens and Petty Tyrants: 108 Metaphors for Mindfulness*. He has over thirty years of clinical practice and experience with yoga and meditation. He has practiced with several spiritual masters and teachers including His Holiness the Dalai Lama, from whom he took the bodhisattva vows in 1985 during a ceremony in Bodhgaya, India. Visit arniekozak.com for information on upcoming workshops. Visit the "Learn" section of Dr. Kozak's site for ten hours of free guided meditations to support your mindfulness practice.

About Wisdom Publications

Wisdom Publications is the leading publisher of classic and contemporary Buddhist books and practical works on mindfulness. Publishing books from all major Buddhist traditions, Wisdom is a nonprofit charitable organization dedicated to cultivating Buddhist voices the world over, advancing critical scholarship, and preserving and sharing Buddhist literary culture.

To learn more about us or to explore our other books, please visit our website at www.wisdompubs.org. You can subscribe to our eNewsletter, request a print catalog, and find out how you can help support Wisdom's mission either online or by writing to:

Wisdom Publications
199 Elm Street
Somerville, Massachusetts 02144 USA

You can also contact us at 617-776-7416 or info@wisdompubs.org.

Wisdom is a 501(c)(3) organization, and donations in support of our mission are tax deductible.

Wisdom Publications is affiliated with the Foundation for the Preservation of the Mahayana Tradition (FPMT).

Also Available
from Wisdom Publications

WILD CHICKENS AND PETTY TYRANTS
108 Metaphors for Mindfulness
Arnie Kozak

"Compelling, entertaining, and useful—
I couldn't put it down!"
—Dr. Steve Taubman, author of *Unhypnosis*

MINDFULNESS IN PLAIN ENGLISH
Bhante Gunaratana

"A classic—one of the very best English sources for
authoritative explanations of mindfulness."
—Daniel Goleman, author of *Emotional Intelligence*

DAILY DOSES OF WISDOM
A Year of Buddhist Inspiration
Edited by Josh Bartok

"Directions: Read one page a day. Can be taken with meal.
Side effects may include insight, compassion, and wisdom.
Stop immediately if experiencing nirvana."
—Sumi Loundon, author of *Blue Jean Buddha*

DON'T WORRY, BE GRUMPY
Inspiring Stories for Making the Most of Each Moment
Ajahn Brahm

"I love a Dharma book that I can open randomly to any page and know I'll find a valuable teaching."
—Toni Bernhard, author of *How to Be Sick*

SAYING YES TO LIFE
(Even the Hard Parts)
Ezra Bayda with Josh Bartok
Foreword by Thomas Moore

"Astonishing."—*Spirituality & Health*

MINDFULNESS WITH BREATHING
A Manual for Serious Beginners
Ajahn Buddhadasa Bhikkhu

"A precious yogic manual."
—Larry Rosenberg, author of *Breath by Breath*

MINDFUL TEACHING AND TEACHING MINDFULNESS
A Guide for Anyone Who Teaches Anything
Deborah Schoeberlein David with Suki Sheth

"A gift for educators, helpful in any classroom, for any teacher, and with every student."
—Goldie Hawn, children's advocate and founder of the Hawn Foundation

MINDFUL MONKEY, HAPPY PANDA
Lauren Alderfer
Illustrated by Kerry Lee MacLean

"This beautiful story shows us all how to dwell peacefully
and happily in the present moment."
—Thich Nhat Hanh

THE MINDFUL WRITER
Noble Truths of the Writing Life
Dinty W. Moore

"Small but powerful—a welcome addition to many writers' desks, and
an inspiring and supportive gift."—*ForeWord*

MINDFULNESS YOGA
The Awakened Union of Breath, Body, and Mind
Frank Jude Boccio
Foreword by Georg Feuerstein

A *Yoga Journal* Editor's Choice